T-SHIRTING

T-SHIRTING

A Do-it-Yourself Guide
to Getting it on Your Chest

by Charles Platt

photographs by Bernard Glickman

HAWTHORN BOOKS, INC.
Publishers / NEW YORK

T-SHIRTING

Library of Congress Catalog Card Number: 75-25307
ISBN: 0-8015-7484-6
1 2 3 4 5 6 7 8 9 10

To Bruce and Ava
   for the germ of the idea;
To Sandy
   for the realization.

CONTENTS

ACKNOWLEDGMENTS ix

INTRODUCTION xi

1 GETTING INTO IT: Shopping for Shirts 3

2 GETTING IDEAS 7
Borrowing from the Media • From Out of
Your Own Head • Op Art and Geometrical
Designs

3 GETTING IT ON: Transferring Designs 18
Tracing Through the Shirt • The Carbon
Paper Method • Stencils and Templates •
The Grid Method • The Pantograph • The
Photographic Method • Transfer Pencils

4 LAYING ON COLOR 31
Marker Pens • Fabric Paint • Markers Versus
Paint • Crayons

5 A DYEING ART: Tie-Dyeing 63
Choosing Designs • Preparation • Tying
Techniques • The Dyeing Process • Tie-
Bleaching • Tie-Spraying

6 SPELLING IT OUT: Lettering 77
Stenciling and Tracing • Hand Lettering

7 SEWN-ON TRIMMINGS 93
Hand Sewing • Machine Sewing

8 THREADLESS TRIMMINGS 114
Iron-Ons • Glitter • Rhinestones and Studs

9 WAXING ENTHUSIASTIC: Batik 125
Suitable Designs • Preparing the T-Shirt • Batik Techniques: Precolored Wax • Batik Techniques: Pre-Colored Wax

10 SILK-SCREENING 139
The Silk Screen: A Simple Stencil • The Plastic Film Method • Liquid Block-Out Methods • The Photographic Method • Starter Kits

11 MORE T-SHIRTING 147

12 CARING FOR YOUR T-SHIRT 151

APPENDIX: Mail-Order Crafts Suppliers and Manufacturers 153

INDEX 159

ACKNOWLEDGMENTS

The author wishes to thank the sales staff of Hudson Army and Navy Store on the Lower East Side in New York City for their weird, erratic, but conscientious assistance; the inscrutable saleswoman on the fourth floor of Pearl Paint on Canal Street in New York City; Ms. Marnie Whelan for her tolerance and restraint; and the following businesses and individuals who provided invaluable help in assembling this book: Frances Alter; Steve and Elaine Berger; Bob and Beverly Brodowsky; Harry Choron; Phil Dobbs; Lisa Drate; Janey Fire; Renée Glickman; Shirley Glickman; Mythology, 370 Columbus Avenue, New York City; Danny Pace; Mary Jo Poole; Patti Pulio; Russell Redmond; Mr. and Mrs. K. Samelson; Ava Sterling; Bruce Sterling; The Top Stop, 210 West 79th Street, New York City; Lynda West; and Ilene Zeifman.

INTRODUCTION

It began with the button.

The 1960s were a time of ferment. They saw the emergence of youth culture, drug culture, black liberation, gay liberation, militant radicals, California communes, a dozen different new life styles. And an arrogant desire to flaunt these styles in the face of conformity.

The pin-on button evolved to meet the needs of the times. It was an instant way to label oneself, broadcast one's orientation of the world, be witty, be aggressive, be sexy, be nonconformist.

But the button was seldom subtle. It could only carry a few words or a symbol. It was seldom visually attractive. And it was a self-conscious device, as conspicuous and blatant as a product label.

Enter the 1970s; exit mini-skirts and flower children. Enter radical chic; exit the self-conscious fervor of the sixties. Enter faded jeans; exit the button. Now, in the second half of the 1970s, there is no doubt that the T-shirt has taken over as a subtle, attractive means of self-expression. Unpretentious, but fashionable. Plain, but with infinite decorative possibilities. A whole new flag to fly; a complete canvas on which to depict one's mood, one's style, one's person.

T-shirt designs are proliferating, from brand names to landscapes in full color, from tourist souvenirs to fashion wear. Inevitably, prices have gone up as quality has increased. A simple screen-printed T-shirt that might have cost a couple of dollars a few years ago is now likely to sell for five or six, and a *really* fashionable hand-painted item can cost you fifty or sixty dollars at a New York City boutique.

Carol Stettner and Michael Amberger of New York City recently added another dimension to the T-shirt craze by forming the Smell This Shirt Company, which utilizes the process of microencapsulation to produce shirts that when scratched emit the odors of any one of their twenty-four stock fragrances—from apple to licorice to orange peels. Naturally, appropriate illustrations accompany the odors, and the company is reportedly working on a new addition to their line: the marijuana T-shirt. In Miami, Florida, a mail-order firm using the label Scratch 'n Smell produces shirts that fill the air with everything from bananas to pickles. The possibilities are endless.

Meanwhile, plain, unadorned T-shirts are still cheap enough. Transforming them yourself from modest, utilitarian clothing into decorative fashion wear requires only some energy, a few ideas, and a little bit of practical knowledge of the processes involved.

If you have the time and energy, we can supply the know-how of the art of T-shirt decoration. Producing your own designs will certainly be easier than you expect; there is a wide choice of media, from paint to embroidery, marker pens to rhinestones, glitter to silk screening, or any combination of these. The sources for inspiration behind your concept are practically inexhaustible: Ponder your favorite record albums and posters; the pages of magazines, books, and comics; the unrealized visions of your mind's eye.

The cost of materials needed to produce your handmade T-shirt will be minimal, and whatever you have to say, saying it with a T-shirt will produce a fun-to-wear art object that is truly your own statement.

T-SHIRTING

1

GETTING INTO IT:
Shopping for Shirts

Whether you plan to paint your T-shirt, embroider it, dye it, print it, appliqué it, batik it, or embellish it with glitter and rhinestones, the quality of the garment itself will limit the success of your efforts. When shopping for T-shirts you should be as discriminating as an artist choosing among different grades of art paper. Cheap T-shirts are a false economy, generally, not only because they are less likely to fit well and maintain their shape when glitter, appliqués, or embroidery are applied, but also because they tend to be of thin fabric that does not take paint well and will absorb and disperse ink like blotting paper.

Your first concern should be to find T-shirts as thickly and tightly woven as possible. We have tried and recommend Jockey, BVD, Fruit of the Loom, and Hanes, the latter being a good bargain for plain white shirts that are a little thin but nevertheless stand up well to paint and ink.

Next, decide on a selection of colors. We suggest you begin with three white shirts and a couple of tinted ones in pale, unobtrusive colors. The stronger or deeper the color of the fabric, the harder it is to cover it with paints or inks. Unfortunately, most BVD and Fruit of the Loom colors (navy and brown, for example) are unsuitable, and the colored shirts in these brands also tend to have pockets, which may interfere with the design you put on the front of the garment. Jockey T-Shirts, however, have no pockets and come in a wide range of colors, their yellow and pale blue being especially ideal for decoration. Remember, too, that if all else fails, Tintex or Rit fabric dye puts you just pennies away from producing T-shirts in the widest range of colors imaginable.

Last, be sure that the T-shirts you buy are not made of nylon; every fabric paint we have seen features a warning that the paint is not fully permanent when applied to nylon, other man-made fibers, and wool. The same seems to be true for marker pen ink.

In practice, shopping for shirts is liable to be a frustrating experience that takes up far more time than you expect. Be prepared to try a number of different stores, searching for the ideal brand, color, size, and style of T-shirt. Even large department stores tend to be not at all conscientious about maintaining a wide range of unadorned T-shirts. But don't despair if shopping becomes trying: five and dime stores have

A typical test shirt used for sampling various paint methods.

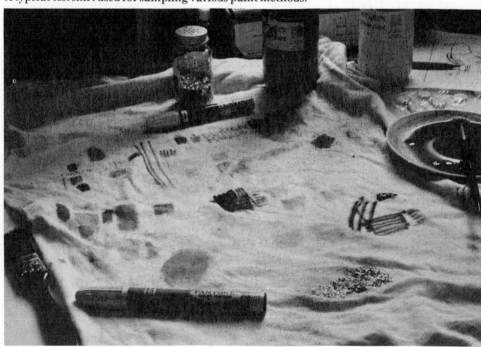

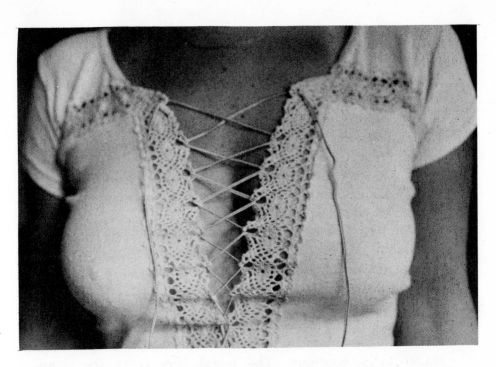

Two T-shirts manufactured by French Maid, San Francisco, California.

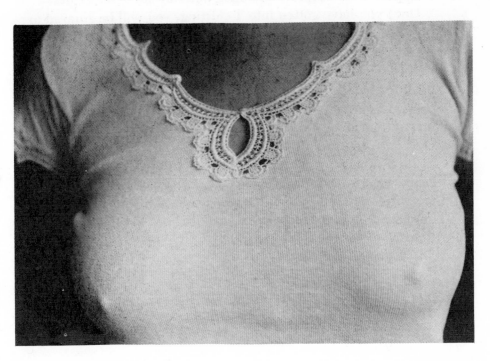

come through for us many times. We suggest that while you're checking out the market you buy one of whatever is immediately available and use it as a test sample. There will be many instances, trying new techniques and materials, when you will need a test shirt, whether to test your drawing skill or the washability of a color. A test shirt used for these purposes can end up looking like an artist's palette, decorated with daubs of color, smudges, lines, bits of embroidery, and patches of glued-on glitter. An art object in itself.

With regard to price, T-shirts are cheap, but if you get hooked on T-shirt art, it can be surprising how many garments your hobby will consume. This being the case, it makes sense to shop where prices are lower. And they do indeed vary. Within large cities the same brand and style of T-shirt can sell for under $2.00 in a five and dime store, $2.50 in a camping or surplus store, $3.00 in a men's clothing store, $4.00 in a department store, and $4.50 in a boutique. The moral here is to try camping/sportswear/surplus stores first, and stay out of boutiques!

Once you have gotten into T-shirting, you will be amazed to find just how common T-shirts are. One major news source recently stated that six out of every ten shirts sold in sportswear stores are some form of T-shirt. The diversity of the T-shirt no doubt is due to the fact that it is available in so many different styles, from the basic T-form to the embroidered ones manufactured by French Maid which are pictured here. One need only flip through the pages of any fashion magazine to find T-shirts with long sleeves, no sleeves, colored collars, button-down fronts, and pockets. While the various styles may be tempting at first, we caution the reader; wait until you have developed some skills before investing in the higher-priced threads.

2
GETTING IDEAS

Borrowing from the Media

What do you want to display on your T-shirt? The techniques described in this book will enable you to put on a name, a slogan, a glittery abstract design, a drawing, a replica of a simple photograph, or a multicolored painting highlighted with embroidery and rhinestones. And the process should not be too much more difficult than, say, painting by numbers.

But where do you start? Anyone with natural artistic ability can sit down and begin sketching ideas, but for the rest of us, it is not so easy. The best way to find inspiration is to go to the media and feel free to borrow. A rock poster, a magazine, a book cover, a piece of fabric, a greeting card, or an art object can produce a wealth of exciting designs. If you're a comics freak, wear your superhero on your chest. It seems that the work of some of the most original artists have been reproduced on record album covers; you might try them. Try also looking in books of works by abstract painters and photography magazines, which often feature very graphic black and white pictures. And don't forget the pop art that is all around you: brand names and package designs of products used at home. Ajax, Budweiser beer, Arm and Hammer baking soda, Kellogg's cereals, Bayer aspirin, Coca-Cola, and, of course, Campbell's soup are all products bearing transferrable designs.

The *Paul McCartney* album inspired this T-shirt. Since white fabric paint does not cover black fabric, the design was painted on a white panel and then sewn to the T-shirt. Iron-on fabric was used for the lettering. Hand painted by Harry Choron.

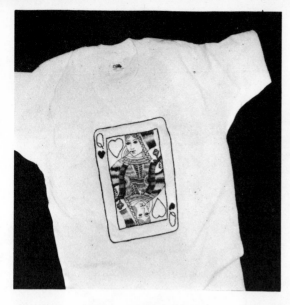

The T-shirt artist is surrounded by unlimited ideas for graphics. This familiar design was copied onto the fabric using the grid method (page 23).

When picking out pictures or designs, you are free to choose samples that are larger or smaller than the design space on the front of a T-shirt. As we will explain in the next chapter, a design can be enlarged or reduced fairly easily when transferring its image to the fabric.

Until you have some previous experience working on T-shirts, try to find designs that are as simple as possible. Ideally they should have clearly defined areas of black (or some solid color) and white. Pictures in which there are gray, intermediate tones will be difficult to trace or sketch on the T-shirt and even more difficult to reproduce with paint. Try to avoid using anything that you can't trace in simple outlines. In the case of photographs, which almost always involve gray areas, you can use a tone-reduction technique to make the image easily transferrable. Survey the picture, and pick out a gray tone that is about halfway between pure white and solid black, then use a fine-point, permanent, black marker to fill in *all* areas of the photograph that are as gray as, or darker than, the tone you have selected. The transferred design will lose some detail but will bring out the picture starkly and simply. Once you have blacked in all the mid- and dark-gray areas, treat the rest of the gray tones as if they are white, and use one of the image transfer techniques described in the next chapter. The illustration here shows a sample photograph before and after tone reduction. The

9

Reducing the tones of a photograph makes it easier to reproduce on a T-shirt.
Left: the original photograph, which includes a range of gray tones. *Right:* the
same photograph after all the mid gray and dark gray tones have been inked
in solid black with a felt marker. The light gray tones were ignored, considered as white, when the picture was blackened. Note that the fuzzy area of
beard has been simplified to a pattern of lines, and the highlights in the hair
have been partly obscured with shading; otherwise, they would have looked
like white holes in the picture. A line has been drawn under the lower lip to
define it, and over the left eye. Great care and precision were needed,
drawing around mouth, nose, and eyes, to preserve the character of the face.
An ultra-fine-point Design Marker was used, plus a broad felt marker for the
large black areas.

more contrast in the photograph to begin with, the easier it will
be to use.

If you decide not to tackle a picture or graphic symbol for
your first project and want to execute some simple lettering
instead, we suggest you read chapter 6 on lettering. Hand-
lettering is a skill it in itself, harder than it looks, especially on
fabric. But there are stencils that make the job simple; and the
sample alphabets supplied in that chapter should aid you.

10

Your last step, before transferring any design to the T-shirt, should be to make a small sketch of how it will look on the garment. Use colored pencils or watercolor markers to suggest the colors you may use. Remember that an idea that seems clever and inspired to you today may seem a lot less creative tomorrow, when some of the initial enthusiasm has subsided, and where T-shirt art is concerned, you will be *wearing* what you produce. So mull over your ideas for a while rather than dive straight in and execute them permanently. Fewer costly and time consuming blunders are made this way.

From Out of Your Own Head

As the previous discussion has pointed out, we are surrounded today by a wealth of artistic ideas. While it may be possible for you to choose one of these and find it an appropriate statement of self-expression, these same artistic sources might just inspire you to create something totally original, a personal statement emanating from your own consciousness. Once you have decided on what sort of statement you care to make, an understanding of the basic elements of design—lines, forms, and composition—will help you to transfer these to paper.

Lines, all by themselves, can express a countless number of things. Look around you for a small sampling: the lines of a rock, buildings, a spider's web, a bolt of lightning, a person's face. They are all different, capturing different moods. You can create a whole painting using variations on a line. Repeated many times, the meaning of a line can be reinforced. You may create tension by juxtaposing an active line, such as the one a ribbon fallen on the floor might make, with a passive line, such as a simple straight one.

Concentrate on your mood. Now try to free associate that feeling with an object and draw the lines that the object brings to mind.

Working with lines, you may find them touching in various places. See where they meet; have you created a form? Once

11

again, allow your thoughts to run free and think in terms of shapes—the soft shape of a rose petal, the restricted shape of a hexagon, and so on. If you think of a shape you would like to see in your design, cut it out of cardboard and place it on your drawing paper. Move it about; experiment with different positions. Cut out four more patterns of the same shape. Does the recurrence of the form reinforce your thought?

Finally, when you have decided on the ingredients of your design, you must give thought to composition—the placement of your lines and forms. Traditionalists prefer symmetrical patterns in which the design is dominated by a focal point, usually occurring in the center, which is surrounded by various other elements. However, you can experiment with asymmetry by cutting your forms from cardboard and placing them on your T-shirt until you have arrived at a pleasing arrangement. You may try dropping them haphazardly on the fabric, overlaying them, or placing them side by side in a straight row.

You can experiment with design elements by sketching on a sheet of paper approximately 8½ by 11 inches (the size of an average T-shirt design). If you draw in ink or bold pencil, you will be able to develop your designs by starting out with one sketch, then laying a new sheet of tracing paper over the first and retracing only those parts of your first sketch that you found satisfactory. Then do over the unsuitable areas. This process can be repeated until the result is perfect—that is, the way you want it to be.

Op Art and Geometrical Designs

These fall halfway between ideas borrowed from the media and ideas that you produce entirely yourself. If you are not particularly talented at art but like the idea of wearing something original, and if you have a steady hand and some patience, geometrical patterns are a good choice. The simplest op art uses alternating areas of black and white (or areas of contrasting colors, such as dark green and bright yellow) to

A simple op-art pattern produced by drawing horizontal and vertical lines between points marked on a circle at intervals of 15 degrees. Alternate squares were blackened, and the design was enclosed in a square to give it a background.

produce illusions of depth, texture, and motion. The designs illustrated here are some examples produced within the area of a circle. Each one was drawn using only straight lines, and connecting points were marked out at regular intervals around the edge of the circle. You will need a full-circle protractor for this, preferably eight inches in diameter, costing only a dollar or two from an art supply store. In some of the designs, the lines only go partway across the area of the circle, but in every case the lines were laid down in a methodical pattern using as guides the regular intervals marked on the circle's edge.

13

A slightly more complex design. Once again, points were marked on a circle at intervals of 15 degrees. This time they were used as guides for the bands of black and white that "step around" the circle. Placing a ruler along the edge of any of the lines in the design will show which two points on the circle edge were used to produce the line.

You can copy any one of the original designs shown here or start experimenting yourself. A circular design looks good on a T-shirt, but experiment with square areas, hexagons, anything you like, dividing their perimeters into equal segments, then drawing lines between pairs of points according to a regular,

The longer you stare at this design, the more its shapes seem to change. Its effect alters also when it is turned sideways or upside down. As with the other op-art patterns, this one was produced by starting with a circle divided into equal 15-degree segments. The construction was far more complex, however, and it would be easier to trace this drawing than reconstruct it geometrically.

systematic rule. For example, try connecting each point to another one ten intervals further around the edge of the figure, counting clockwise. Try subdividing the areas that you produce. Try erasing line segments. Notice how a pattern of lines may look very dull until you fill in alternate areas with dark ink, which will intensify the whole design.

As in the design on page 13, horizontal and vertical lines were drawn between points marked on a circle at intervals of 15 degrees. Some segments of these lines were omitted to form the final pattern, however, and additional lines were drawn diagonally across the circle.

You can reproduce a design on the the T-shirt fabric by simply pencil marking the circle (or other shape) that the design is drawn within, then drawing directly on the fabric with fine-point markers. This method will require the use of a mounting board, which is described in the next chapter, and chapter 4, "Laying on Color," will supply complete information on the use of marker pens.

3

GETTING IT ON:
Transferring Designs

After you find a picture or design that you like or have evolved one in your imagination, you are ready to transfer it to the T-shirt, then bring it to life with paint, ink, embroidery, or whatever medium you choose. The question is how to make the transfer.

Impatience and enthusiasm may tempt you simply to place your design or sketch beside the T-shirt and copy it right onto the fabric with paintbrush or marker pen. It takes courage to work this way—probably more courage than sense! There are seven different easy ways to transfer a design from its source to the T-shirt in the form of faint guidelines, and we strongly suggest that you lay down the paintbrush for a moment and consider using one of the following.

Tracing Through the Shirt

This is the simplest and quickest technique. White T-shirts are often made of material that is thin enough for you to see the outlines of a bold design placed directly underneath the fabric. If your design is bold and clear and is the same size as you want it on the T-shirt, push it *inside* the garment and shuffle it around until it is in the correct position. The T-shirt should be laid out flat, not stretched or distorted in any way. Lay a long ruler or straight piece of wood across the shirt, from the bottom of the

18

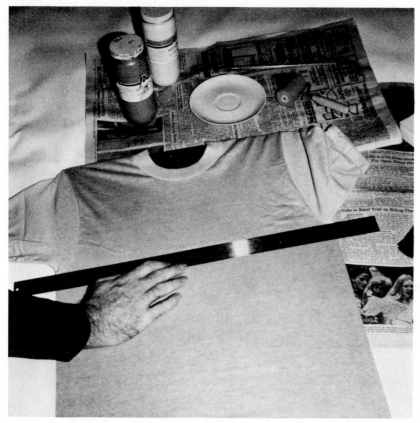

Lay a long ruler across the shirt from the bottom of one sleeve to the bottom of the other in order to establish a horizontal guide.

left sleeve to the bottom of the right sleeve. Make sure that any horizontal lines in your design are parallel with this line, between the two sleeves.

Beware of placing the design too low on the T-shirt. The center of the design should be high on the chest when the garment is worn. Check for correct placement in advance by holding your design in position and looking at yourself in a mirror. A good working rule is that the top edge of any design should be only about three inches below the neck opening of the T-shirt. Make that five or six inches if the design is small.

Once you are ready to begin tracing the design through the T-shirt material, the major consideration is securing the fabric so

19

that it does not shift during the process. If your design is on paper, make a cardboard backing for it, then carefully fold the T-shirt fabric around the edges so that the design is sandwiched between the fabric and the cardboard behind it. Add paper clips (Hunt clips are ideal for this) on all four sides. If you are using ordinary paper clips, you can prevent the wire ends of the clips from damaging the fabric by using little slips of paper between the fabric and the clips. Set the assembly on a firm, level surface and experiment lighting it from different directions, making certain the design shows through the T-shirt as clearly as possible. Then make one last check that the fabric is not distorted; the lines of stitching should be straight, without any curves or kinks.

If your design is not on paper (one might use a round container or even a vase for T-shirt art inspiration) there will be a problem laying the fabric over the design. You might consider tracing the design first onto tracing paper, inking it in boldly, and then using this (with white paper behind it, to make the design show up) as your original for tracing through the T-shirt.

A very important caution: some of the coloring processes described in this book do not have very much covering power. This means they will not entirely conceal pencil lines that you make on the shirt while tracing your design. Consequently, use a very soft pencil (2B or 3B) with a smooth, rounded point rather than a sharp point that will leave blacker lines and tend to dig into the fabric. Press *very* lightly, making the faintest possible lines. The only exception to this rule is where you are planning to embroider the design or go over it with dark paint, ink, or glitter. This, of course, will conceal pencil on the fabric completely.

The Carbon Paper Method

If your design is not easily visible through the T-shirt, the carbon paper method is the next easiest for transferring the image. For this method, your design must be the same size as it will appear on the shirt and must be on a loose sheet of paper. If you are borrowing a picture from a book, record sleeve, or whatever, make a tracing of it on tracing paper, then use this copy in the following process.

Lay out the T-shirt and place on it, in correct position, the paper bearing your design. Slide a sheet of carbon paper, black side down, between the paper and the T-shirt. Cut from any old cardboard box a piece of corrugated cardboard that is the same size as your design. Push the cardboard inside the T-shirt until it is exactly behind the design. Check the positioning again, then fold the T-shirt around and behind the cardboard, on all four sides, taking care not to stretch the fabric or distort it. Finally, attach Hunt clips (or paper clips with slips of paper to protect the fabric) all around the edges. The clips should firmly anchor the design, carbon paper, T-shirt, and backing cardboard all together in a fat sandwich.

Now use a ball-point pen to trace over your design. Choose a colored ink, so you can see where you've traced. Peek under one corner of the carbon paper to check that the design is transferring properly. As when using a soft pencil, the marks on the T-shirt should be as faint as possible. Incidentally, mistakes cannot be erased (the marks made by carbon paper are surprisingly permanent), so draw carefully and avoid pressing with any hard object, such as your hand. Pressure is transmitted by the carbon paper in the form of unwanted black smudges.

An alternative way of setting up the T-shirt for the carbon paper method is to lay the shirt out flat on a firm, smooth surface and secure your design and carbon paper to the fabric with Scotch tape. The advantage of this method is that you can easily check to see if your design is in the correct position and horizontal on the garment because the T-shirt is laid out flat instead of being folded around and behind the cardboard backing. However, the first method does hold the fabric more securely than the Scotch tape method, and removing the tape from the T-shirt may damage it slightly, pulling some of the threads.

Stencils and Templates

If your design is extremely simple and graphic, you may be able to put its main elements on thin cardboard or very stout paper in the form of a stencil or template. Designs in which the same shape is repeated several times are ideal for this process. Cut out or around the shapes you require, preferably using an artist's knife for greater precision than is possible with scissors. We recommend a No. 199 Stanley knife, which has a large body, enabling it to be gripped firmly, and uses disposable, razor-sharp, pointed blades. It is sold in most art supply stores or is available by mail order from the art retailers listed in the Appendix of this book.

Once you have your shapes in cardboard or thick paper, draw around them gently with a 2B (or softer) pencil while holding the shapes down on the T-shirt with your free hand. Alternatively, in the case of stencils, go ahead and apply paint through them. Chapter 6 contains a comprehensive discussion of painting techniques suitable for stencils.

Cut stencil and template shapes with an artist's knife.

A simple stenciled design can be repeated for an interesting effect. This design lends itself to repetition. The T-shirt was painted in undiluted water-base paint using a commercially made stencil.

The Grid Method

This is a method for enlarging or reducing the size of a design. It is best suited to simple designs; for complex designs, the photographic method (p. 27) is easier.

Using a triangle or protractor, draw a square or rectangle around the design that you want to transfer. Then divide this area into a lot of small squares like a checkerboard, using a very sharp pencil or a fine-point, ball-point pen. To be sure that all

Enlarging a design using the grid method.

the squares are equal in size, use a ruler to measure out their intervals along each edge of the area. If you do not wish to mark the original copy of the design, trace it, then lay out the checkerboard grid on your tracing, instead.

Next, decide how big the design is going to be on the T-shirt. Take a piece of paper large enough to accommodate this size (tape two pieces of paper together, if necessary) and draw a square or rectangle. If a rectangle is used, it must be in *exactly* the same proportion as the rectangle you have drawn on your original design. If your original rectangle is 1½ times as wide as it is high, then the one you draw on paper must also be in these proportions. If your original rectangle is, say four by six inches, the one you draw could be eight by twelve inches, or ten by fifteen inches, and so on.

Divide the second rectangle (or square) into exactly the same number of checkerboard squares as you did on the original design. Then, using a pencil so that mistakes can be erased, transfer the original design one square at a time. By dividing it up this way, you will be able to copy it square for square, without fear of distorting its overall shape and form, and the simplicity of the design within each square should enable you to draw it without too many problems.

When you have copied the design to your satisfaction, use the carbon paper method (pp. 20–21) to transfer it to your T-shirt.

The Pantograph

The pantograph is an old-fashioned artist's aid that is still useful for transferring a simple design, enlarging or reducing it at the same time.

The gadget is a linkage of four wooden or metal arms, as illustrated here. To copy a design and enlarge it in the process, the end of one arm of the pantograph is anchored. It is usually mounted on a block that can be clamped to a drawing board or tabletop. A pencil is mounted in the end of the other arm of the pantograph. Midway between, the bottom joint of the linkage is

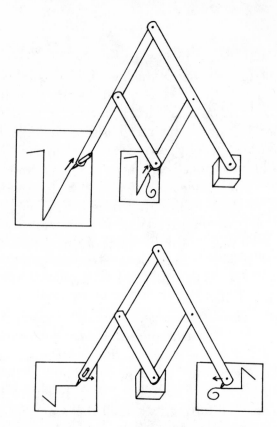

The *top* illustration shows the pantograph doubling the size of a design. The end of its right arm is anchored but allowed to pivot; a pencil is mounted on the end of the left arm; and there's a joint midway between the two arms carrying a pointer. The pointer is tracing the lines of the small design in the center, and the pencil copies the motions of the pointer. If the positions of pointer and pencil are interchanged, the contours traced by the pointer will be reproduced by the pencil *half*-size.

The *bottom* illustration shows the pantograph with the middle joint anchored but allowed to pivot. One arm carries the pencil, the other carries the pointer. The design traced by the pointer is now reproduced same-size by the pencil, although it is turned upside down in the process.

Dots on the struts of the pantograph indicate pivoting points. If the reader constructs a pantograph, it is essential for the left arm and right arm to be equal in length and for the two shorter arms to be equal to one another. Looseness in the joints must not be allowed. A suitable length for left and right arms is one foot, or thirty inches if larger designs are to be produced. The two shorter arms are each half the length of the longer arms. If constructing the device from hardwood, use 1-by-¼ inch and sheet metal screws, which can be driven into small holes drilled at the pivot points. (Bolts can be substituted, provided they are secured with locknuts to prevent them working loose.) It is easier to construct two separate pantographs than one that will adapt either to the configuration in the top or bottom illustrations.

extended down in the form of a pointer, which is traced carefully over the design that is to be copied. The linkage works so that each movement of the pointer is amplified and reproduced faithfully by the pencil, producing a result that is twice the size of the original design. By exchanging the positions of pencil and pointer, a design can be copied and reduced to half its size.

The pantograph can also be used to make same-size copies if the anchored point is at the middle joint of the linkage and pencil and pointer are mounted at the ends of the two arms. A same-size copy produced in this way will of course be no better than a tracing made with tracing paper, but the pantograph is a quick way to put the design on a T-shirt, since the pencil can be positioned to draw directly on the fabric itself. To reduce the tendency of the pencil point to snag in the T-shirt cloth, stretch the shirt (as described in the next section) and use a pencil with a smooth, rounded tip.

Pantographs are no longer sold widely, but they can still be found in some art supply stores; and anyone at all handy at carpentry can easily make one with struts of wood and screws.

The Photographic Method

This is a simple method but does require some equipment and more preparation than the other techniques. If you own a camera that will focus at a distance of three feet (or less) and will take film that produces color slides, and if you have a projector for displaying these color slides, you are ready to begin.

In bright light, photograph the design or picture that you want to transfer to the T-shirt. Bring the camera as close as you can, so that the design is as large as possible in the viewfinder. When the film has been processed, use a slide projector to cast your photograph onto a T-shirt, which acts as the screen. By moving the projector closer to the T-shirt, you can make the design smaller on the screen. Move the projector farther away and the design will grow larger. Once it is the size you want, you can duck around the projector beam and trace the design in soft

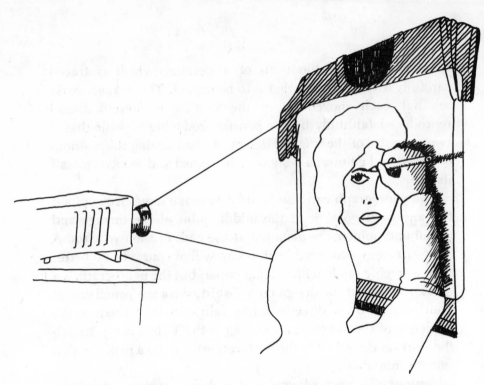

Transferring an image to a T-shirt with the photographic technique. The T-shirt is mounted over a backing board and placed at a distance from the slide projector that results in the design appearing in the desirable size on the fabric. The outline of the projected image is then traced onto the fabric with a soft pencil. It may be necessary to turn on the room lights occasionally to check the results that are being produced.

pencil on the shirt. The accompanying figure illustrates the technique.

This system has a couple of disadvantages. There is the cost of the color film to be considered and the irritating time one has to wait while the film is being processed. However, it allows faithful reproduction of designs from all kinds of sources without marking the originals in any way and also allows their size to be freely enlarged or reduced on the T-shirt.

To support the T-shirt vertically while the picture is being projected onto it, a large backing board is needed. This is slid inside the shirt so that the fabric is stretched slightly, over and around it. You can use corrugated cardboard, but Masonite (available cheaply at any lumberyard) is better. It should be cut

28

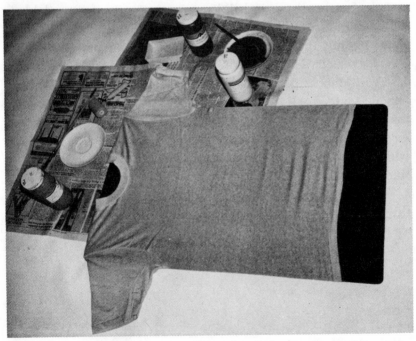

The backing board with its rounded corners is inserted into the T-shirt. The board should be two inches wider than the shirt when it is layed out flat, and it should be long enough to accommodate the entire length of the shirt.

to measure two inches wider than the width of the T-shirt when the fabric is laid out, unstretched. The top corners of the board must be rounded off to allow it to be pushed inside the T-shirt without snagging the fabric. It should be tall enough to support the entire length of the T-shirt.

This backing board is recommended also for use while the T-shirt is being painted or drawn on in ink. It holds the garment firmly without paper clips and provides a good, smooth surface to work on. Although it does distort the fabric slightly, stretching it more horizontally than vertically, this distortion is un-noticeable unless geometrical figures, such as circles or squares, are going to be in a design.

Transfer Pencils

Transfer pencils, or indelible copying pencils, are available in many sewing supply stores as well as from mail-order suppliers listed in the Appendix. Draw your design on paper with the transfer pencil. Then place the T-shirt on a flat surface, making sure you smooth out all wrinkles in the fabric. Pin the drawing, penciled side down, to the fabric, carefully placing the design in the desired position on the T-shirt. While your iron is at the cotton setting, iron the paper slowly. Peek under the paper while you iron; your design should be transferred within about thirty seconds.

Your lines will be dark and, of course, indelible. Therefore, this techniques is best used for designs in which outlines will eventually be fully covered.

4
LAYING ON COLOR

A painting on canvas may be labeled Do Not Touch, hung behind glass, and usually protected from direct sunlight. But a painting on a T-shirt is liable to be subjected to routine wear and tear in which the fabric is flexed, rubbed, wrinkled, perspired into, subjected to all kinds of weather, and finally washed in detergent that is specifically designed to remove any form of stain or pigmentation.

Not many forms of paint, ink, or dye will stand up to this treatment. In case you are tempted to experiment, we can assure you that we have tested all of the following possibilities and have found them unsuitable.

Drawing inks. Though they may be labeled waterproof, in our experience they lose at least half their intensity in just one wash.

Acrylic paint. Acrylics are available in an exciting selection of premixed colors. They are water soluble, quick drying, and can, indeed, be applied to fabric. Our experience, however, indicates that unless they are used in thick coats, the designs wash out almost completely in the course of laundering. The techniques required for acrylic fabric painting, then, are best left to the experienced artist.

Artists' oil paint. This is slow drying, and after it has dried, it tends to crack when the fabric is flexed.

Household oil paint. This suffers the same drawbacks as artists' oil paint and in addition tends to spread into the fabric when it is applied, making precise work impossible.

31

Marker pen design on three-color background. By Billye of Mahogany Productions, The Top Stop, New York City.

Household water-base paint. Another washout.

Ball-point pen ink. Easily applied, precise, and fast drying, but it fades a surprising amount even when hand washed in cold water.

Printers' ink. Wateproof, durable, flexible, but hard to obtain in small quantities and too viscous to be easily applied.

Our conclusion is that the two kinds of coloring most successful in fabric work are permanent-ink marker pens and paints specifically designed for fabric application. (Fabric crayons, which are also suitable, are discussed at the end of this chapter.) The marker pens do fade a little bit but are very easy to work with; the fabric paints are truly permanent but require more skill in application. We will deal with the markers first.

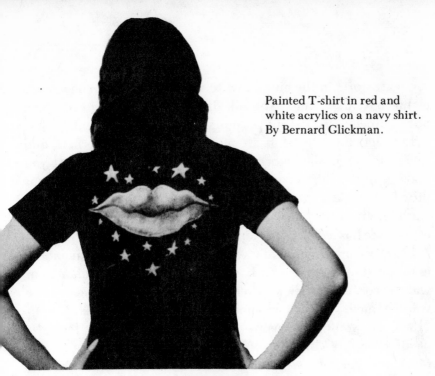

Painted T-shirt in red and white acrylics on a navy shirt. By Bernard Glickman.

Marker Pens

Any janitor or cleaning person can testify that graffiti written in Magic Marker is almost impossible to remove. The graffiti problem on New York City subways has become so severe that

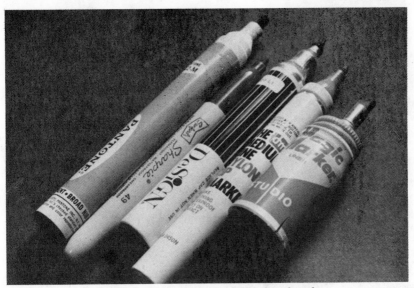

A selection of permanent markers. Note the different nib styles.

some art stores in the city refuse to sell markers to anyone under eighteen years of age. The ink dries instantly and resists even abrasive cleansers; for our purposes, then, it sounds ideal.

In practice, some colors are more permanent than others, and some marker brands work better than others. We suggest you make a test T-shirt of your own, writing the names of various different markers on it in their respective inks. After it has been washed, apply new ink beside the old for comparison. Our own experience has led us to the following conclusions.

First, be sure that the marker you buy contains permanent ink as opposed to water-base ink. It should be labeled permanent or waterproof, and when you remove the cap, it should give off a volatile smell. (Water-base markers are virtually odorless.)

Second, you must realize that there has been a fantastic proliferation of brands, colors, and nib styles since Magic Markers first appeared more than a decade ago. Brands that we have tested include Sharpie, Design Marker, Dri Mark, and Pantone, as well as the old, original Magic Marker. All of them

This T-shirt combines three processes: spray painting for the background, marker pen drawing for the outline, and fabric painting for the coloring. The Top Stop, New York City.

are available in nib styles that are firm and capable of drawing fine lines. The cheapest of them, Sharpie, comes in a limited range of bright, basic colors, some of which are quite permanent (black, blue), others tending to wash out (especially red*, which fades to a sickly pink after a few washings). The nib is of a medium-hard fiber that tends to wear down and become blunt when used on fabric; however, it can be sharpened with the careful use of a razor blade or artist's knife. Sharpie is widely distributed in stationery stores as well as art stores, and, though smaller than some of the other pens, has at least enough ink capacity to fill in a couple of average T-shirt designs.

*We're not kidding, folks!

Using fine-point lines, this felt-tipped pen design depicts San Francisco. By Bruce Sterling.

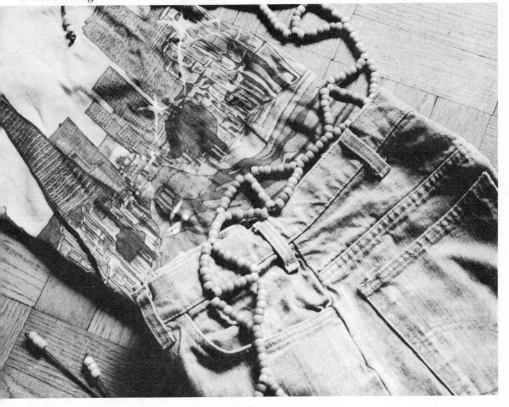

Dri Mark is probably the next most widely distributed, after Sharpie, and is quite reasonably priced. There is a wide range of colors and three nib styles: wide (felt tip, suitable only for large areas of color or bold lines), medium (nylon tip), and fine (nylon tip). On the average, Dri Mark colors seem slightly more permanent than Sharpies.

Design Markers have an even better permanance than Dri Mark, the black ink being excellent. Also, the pens are available in four nib styles, including ultrafine, making them ideal for delicate work. They are generally only sold in art supply stores.

The Pantone markers provide the most permanent of inks we have used but are not widely distributed and are by far the most expensive of the pens tested. There is a very wide range of colors and a choice of nibs.

Lastly, the original Magic Marker. An interesting feature of their line is the flourescent set, which we have not tested and leave to your own sense of adventure. No longer dominating the marker market and by no means the cheapest of the markers available, we have had disappointing results where its permanence is concerned. However, it is more than likely that some ink colors fade less than others; we therefore urge you to make your own tests to discover your own preferences.

The following table is an approximate rating based on testing a limited number of samples. Different colored inks of any one brand may show different degrees of permanence, and prices

Table of Features of Selected Permanent Marking Pens

Pen	Approximate Cost	Choice of Colors	Choice of Nib Styles	Color Permanence
Sharpie	49¢	10	1	poor
Dri Mark	69¢	12	3	fair
Magic Marker	90¢	192*	3	poor
Design Marker	80¢	96*	4	good
Pantone	$1.20	96*	2	very good

* Color selection varies among the nib styles.

may vary. Our test consisted of a cold-water wash in a washing machine with laundry detergent, followed immediately by tumble drying. The test was performed three times on each brand of marker, and successive fading was noted.

SUITABLE DESIGNS

Because most markers are available with fine points, they are ideal for drawing narrow, precise lines. Examples are the outlines of hand lettering, pictures involving a lot of detail, and

The "Dr. Gzorninplatz, I presume?" shirt was drawn in marker pens by Phil Dobbs. The garish combination of colors (turquoise, violet, and brown on a yellow T-shirt) emphasizes the subject matter.

Marker pen design by Sandra Choron.

cartoon-type drawings. Furthermore, the wide ranges of colored pens available make them suitable for shaded illustrations.

The main limitation of markers is in covering large areas. A broad-tipped marker will allow you to fill in an area of color quite quickly, but you may be disappointed to find that what looked like a solid area becomes a blotchy, uneven area after washing. Our recommendation is to use paints for large solid-colored areas and markers for adding lines and detail.

Where should you look for design ideas for marker pens? A Beardsley drawing, a Peanuts cartoon, a scene from a comic book, an op art design, most forms of graphic art.

In all aspects of T-shirt decoration, we cannot overemphasize the importance of planning ahead. Wasted time and materials can lead to frustration. Therefore, throughout this book, please pay special attention to the instructions for preparing T-shirts.

If you are expecting to color your design with marker pens, remember that many marker ink colors are very transparent; they do not have have much covering power and will tend to allow the penciled outline of your design to show through. Consequently, when transferring the design to the T-shirt (as described in chap. 3), you should use very light pencil strokes or press very gently on carbon paper if you are using the carbon paper method (see pp. 20–21).

While marker ink has a slight tendency to spread into T-shirt fabric (the blotting paper effect), this tendency is minimized if you draw on a colored T-shirt as opposed to a white one. The fibers of the colored shirt are less able to absorb ink, since they have already been saturated with dye. If you must use a white shirt, make it Hanes. As we have mentioned in chapter 2, these have the least tendency to produce the blotting paper effect.

Once you have the T-shirt ready with the design traced upon it, you will need a backing board over which the shirt must be stretched (see p. 29). A board of Masonite is ideal, since it

The blotting paper effect. The fabric has soaked up ink from the marker and is now dispersing it. The marker was held in steady contact with the fabric for just five seconds. A word to the wise, we trust, is sufficient.

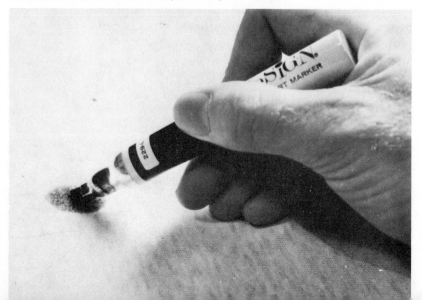

Felt-tipped markers and fabric paint were used on this T-shirt made by Mahogany Productions, The Top Stop, New York City.

provides a hard, smooth surface. After you have the T-shirt stretched evenly over the board and centered on it, no further preparations are necessary.

DRAWING TECHNIQUES

The main difficulty you are likely to encounter is the tendency of the marker tips to dig into the fabric instead of stroking over it. This problem is especially irritating when using markers with very fine points. Having the T-shirt fabric stretched over its backing board helps, but in addition you will need to press as lightly and delicately as possible, holding the pen at as small an angle to the fabric as you can. Lastly, use a finger of your free hand to anchor the fabric a couple of inches from the spot where you are working and try to draw lines away from your anchoring finger rather than toward it.

If your design uses a variety of colors, apply the lightest shades first. Rest your drawing hand on a piece of clean scrap paper so

When drawing on fabric with a fine-point marker, anchor the fabric with your free hand and then draw away from that hand.

Marker pen design. The drawing was taken from a greeting card. The balloons were shaded in various shades of red, green, and blue. By Sandra Choron.

that your skin does not pick up and redeposit traces of ink from areas of the T-shirt that you have just worked on. Likewise, be sure that the fingers of your free hand do not accumulate ink traces that will be transferred back onto the fabric as smudges where you hold it down.

When filling in an area, shade the color from the center of the area out toward its edge, but stop a fraction of an inch away from the edge, and wait a full minute to check whether the marker ink is going to spread out in the fabric. If it doesn't, you can draw right up to the edge of the area.

42

Felt markers were used around the hand lettering for a shaded, dramatic effect. The orange T-shirt with its red and purple lettering produces an authentic comic-book impression.

Shading with marker ink.

It is generally difficult to make a clear, clean division between two adjoining colors of roughly equal intensity (such as bright blue and bright green). Either try to arrange your design so that dark colors adjoin light colors, or use a fine-pointed black marker to add a clear dividing line after the colors have been applied.

If your design incorporates straight lines, be especially sure that the fabric is evenly stretched over its backing. Check that the lines of stitching are vertical and free from wiggles. Then press down as firmly as you can with your ruler and as lightly as you can with the marker. Wipe the ruler immediately after use to remove ink residues that will otherwise accumulate.

It is possible to add shading with a marker pen almost as if it were a pencil on paper. Making quick strokes, decrease the pressure of the pen point on the cloth during the course of each stroke; a fading-out effect will be produced. This technique was used in the Shazam T-shirt shown on page 43.

Fabric Paint

Handicraft stores often sell complete fabric painting kits containing small portions of various paint colors, brushes, instructions, and in some cases, such as the Flo-Paque kit, sample designs and patterns that you can follow in case you have no ideas of your own.

We do not recommend the kits for three reasons: they are very expensive for the quantity of paint they provide; the brushes are generally poor; and the unnecessarily large range of colors is liable to leave you with some colors exhausted after painting just a couple of T-shirts while others are left hardly touched. As we will explain in the section on color mixing, the only colors you will need to produce any color in the spectrum are the three primaries plus black and white. These you can buy by the jar from a well-stocked art supply store. (See the Appendix for mail-order suppliers in case you are not conveniently close to a large art supply store.) A typical price for fabric paint is $2.50 for sixteen ounces of paint—enough to cover dozens of T-shirts.

Of the fabric paints we have tested, we recommend two brands as being easy to work with, truly permanent, and reasonably priced. One, Versatex, is water based, which means that water can be used for diluting the paint (within limits) and for cleaning paint brushes and spills. The other brand, Prang, is an oil-base paint requiring turpentine for cleanup. Both these paints contain a special ingredient that is activated by heat after the paint has dried, making the color resisitant to washing . The heat can be applied with an iron or by placing the T-shirt in an oven for a few minutes. We recommend the former method.

VERSATEX VERSUS PRANG

Water-base paint is easier to work with than oil base. Brushes are easily washed, and stray smudges on hands or furniture come off easily with soap and water. The painted fabric dries in less than an hour and can then be ironed (with the iron set at cotton on its temperature scale) for three or four minutes to activate the

Fabric paint will become permanent when heat is applied by an iron set at cotton. It is advisable to use a sheet of tracing paper to protect the paint and shirt from the surface of the iron.

colors' permanence ingredient. Manufacturers instruct the artist not to iron directly over the painted area, so we suggest placing a sheet of tracing paper over the face of the painted design and ironing over this. Likewise, ironing the back of the design will ensure the longevity of your shirt.

Versatex is odorless and nontoxic. It is semiopaque, meaning that it will *partially* conceal the color of a T-shirt that has already been dyed. The paint can be diluted with Versatex extender, which makes the paint color paler and less opaque but does not thin the consistency of the paint; or you can use water, which thins both the color and the consistency. If water is used, the instructions recommend adding Versatex binder to insure that the diluted paint does not lose some of its permanence.

Prang oil-base paint is less opaque than Versatex and comes out of the jar in a slightly thinner consistency that some may find easier to work with. It also seems to penetrate into the cloth more readily. It dries faster then Versatex, reducing the chances of smudging work that one has completed; this quick-drying quality is especially useful when using stencils. On the other hand, the manufacturers recommend leaving the completed paint job for twenty-four hours before ironing it.

Like Versatex, Prang makes an extender for diluting the colors. This looks like white paint, and it can be hard to tell its exact effect on a color until after the color has dried. We found it easier to dilute Versatex, although any paint on fabric will tend to dry a slightly different color compared to the way it looks when wet. Fabric itself looks darker when wet than when dry.

Although Prang is less convenient to wash out of brushes and off hands, it does respond adequately to plain, simple turpentine—probably more easily than most house paints. The traces of turpentine that remain in brushes and on skin after cleaning up can be removed with dishwashing liquid.

Prang paints are toxic, and there is a caution about breathing their vapor for long periods without adequate ventilation. Thus, they are not suitable for young children.

On balance we feel that a water-base paint has more advantages than an oil-base paint, although the texture and transparency of Prang colors make it slightly more pleasant to work with. One's preference is largely a matter of taste, and you should try a sample of each before deciding for yourself.

SUITABLE DESIGNS

Fabric paints are thick in consistency and designed not to spread out fuzzily into the fibers of the fabric. Thus, it is possible to produce clean, sharp-edged designs with them—in theory. In practice, the flexible tip of a paint brush and the thick consistency of the paint make it difficult to produce fine lines or detail work.

Paints are best suited to bold designs featuring large slabs of color. They also offer the fascinating possibilities of color mixing and blending, producing an infinite range of tones and shades. When thinned with extender, the paint can be used to create a misty, multi-hued background over which a foreground subject can be drawn with, for example, a black marker pen.

Photographs that have been reduced to stark black and white (see chap. 3 for a full description of this technique) are ideal for execution in paint, since they often involve fairly simple shapes and lack detail. Instead of reproducing them in black and white, try red and pale blue or (more garishly) dark green and orange.

Acrylic paint design by Bernard Glickman.

The author's Knife-in-the-Back T-shirt was done in fabric paint.

Abstract designs, with the exception of op art and similarly fussy patterns requiring a lot of precision, are also good for paint, especially if some blending of colors is involved. As an exercise, try a simple rainbow, curving from one shoulder down to the bottom of the shirt. Apply adjacent colors separately, then blend them on the fabric before they dry, using extender to keep them moist if necessary.

Finger painting, block printing, homemade stenciling, and spray painting are techniques that naturally require fabric paint, but these are discussed in more detail further on in this chapter.

Again, posters make good sources for painted design ideas. You might also consider simply printed fabric, greetings cards, magazine covers, and the ever-useful record jackets. The bold and simple logos or trademarks taken from packages of products such as household cleaners (Ajax) or food (corn flakes) are easily translated into wild and wonderful painted shirts.

48

As when working with marker pens, the shirt should be stretched slightly to minimize the tendency of the fabric to bunch up while it is being worked on. Use a cardboard or Masonite backing, as previously described (see p. 29). In addition, you should slide several thicknesses of newspaper between the shirt and the backing, to absorb surplus paint that will seep through the shirt. If this surplus is not absorbed, it will redeposit itself on the inside of the T-shirt and soak back through to the front in unwanted places.

The manufacturers of fabric paint strongly recommend that the T-shirt be washed and dried before paint is applied to it. This is to remove sizing that may otherwise interfere with the permanence of the paint. We also suggest you wear the T-shirt for a few hours before working on it so that any stretching of the fabric will occur before it is painted rather than afterward.

Make sure that the T-shirt is centered on its backing board and not distorted in any way. Lay out newspapers to catch paint spills; provide yourself with white saucers in which to mix paint colors and a good light source (daylight if possible); and begin.

PAINTING TECHNIQUES

Color mixing. Memories of high school art classes may tell you that the primary paint colors are red, yellow, and blue. This is not strictly true. The real primaries are magenta (a purplish red), lemon or canary yellow (a pale but bright yellow, lighter than golden yellow or chrome yellow), and sky blue. These are the colors that printers use to reproduce full color. In combination with black (to produce somber, shaded tones) and white (to produce pastel shades) they can be mixed to match any color in the spectrum. The table below gives some indication of the results you can expect from mixing various quantities of these, but the percentages are approximate and may vary according to the brand of paint used. We suggest you pour out a small

Approximate Guide to Color Mixing

PERCENTAGE (BY VOLUME) OF EACH PRIMARY IN THE MIXTURE			RESULTING COLOR
YELLOW	MAGENTA	SKY BLUE	
90	10	–	Golden Yellow
60	40	–	Orange
30	70	–	Tomato red
–	30	70	Deep blue
–	60	40	Violet
20	–	80	Aquamarine
50	–	50	Grass green
80	–	20	Yellow–green
55	35	10	Rust brown
45	10	45	Olive green
33	33	33	Brown-black

quantity of each into a separate dish, then experiment, blending them onto some scrap paper. When mixing colors, it is easiest to start with a large quantity of the lighter color and add just a little of the darker, then a little more, mixing thoroughly all the time, until the desired tone is reached. Add magenta to yellow, sky blue to magenta, sky blue to yellow. It is always easier to darken a color than it is to backtrack and try to lighten it. A small amount of a third color to any two-color mix will darken the mix toward brown.

When mixing paint for use on fabric, always mix about twice as much as you think you will need. Fabric absorbs large amounts of paint, and the color changes slightly as it dries, so that if you run out of paint before the job is finished, it will be hard for you to mix more paint to match the original color exactly.

Brushes. A cheap brush won't hold its shape, will lose bristles, will make precise work impossible, and altogether will be a false

A selection of paint brushes. *Left*: small bristle filbert; *center*: large bristle filbert; *right*: watercolor sable.

economy. We strongly suggest you start out with a genuine sable watercolor brush, suitable for filling in large areas (it has a thick body) and also for painting precise lines (it tapers to a point). The bristle segment should be around an inch long and not less than a quarter inch in diameter. This may seem too large a brush for precise work but in practice is ideal for fabric use.

For stencil work, you can use a bristle filbert brush. Its bristles are arranged in a flat, wedge shape and are stiff.

For your first project, choose a simple design on a white T-shirt. Use bold colors with a lot of contrast between them. Thoroughly load your brush with paint and experiment onto some scrap paper to see whether the paint needs to be diluted a little in order to flow well. If it does, this dilution should be made before you begin working on the T-shirt.

Apply lighter colors first and try to work from the top of the T-shirt down toward the bottom. If this is not possible, you may find it is convenient to use a hair dryer to speed up the drying time of the paint so that you can rest your hand on previously painted areas without fear of smudging them. Set the hair dryer to its hottest temperature and hold it an inch from the fabric, moving it slowly to and fro, until you see the paint lose its wet look. Note that the heat of the dryer will partially or wholly activate the ingredient in the fabric paint that makes it permanent. This means that it will no longer be possible to mix new paint onto the fabric with the old, and any mistakes will be impossible to wash out (if you are using water-base paint) or remove with turpentine (if you are using an oil-base paint). So be sure the painted effect is the one wanted before applying hot-air drying.

A simple design easily drawn with marker pens but also well suited for movable stencils or silk-screening. Black ink on a white shirt.

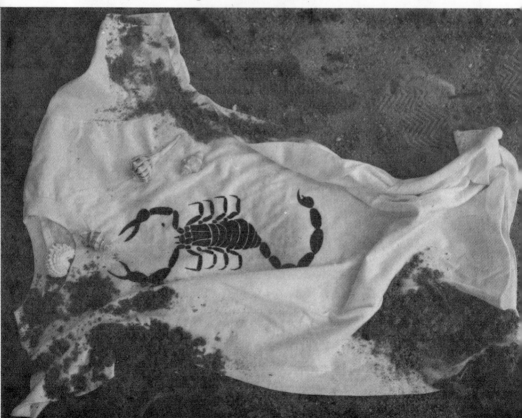

The figure was painted in oil-base paint, heavily diluted with extender where necessary. The barbells were executed in undiluted black paint, and marker pens were used to outline the figure and for detail.

Regarding the techniques of handling a paint brush, blending colors, matching colors, and all the other aspects of the skill of painting, we could continue for many pages. But there are already excellent books on this subject, just as relevant to painting on cloth as to painting on paper or canvas. If you experience difficulty controlling the paintbrush and achieving the results you want, we suggest you consult one of these standard guides.

Once you get the hang of applying the paint to fabric, branch out into more ambitious areas. Experiment by applying different paint colors to different fabric colors, observing how the apparent color of the paint changes as it dries. Add more white to the paint to give it greater density and covering power (although Prang manufacturers caution that using a lot of white reduces the permanence of their paint). With water-base paint, experiment with the wet-on-wet technique. This entails thoroughly soaking the cloth with water, then applying diluted paint, producing beautifully shaded, fuzzy effects reminiscent of some Japanese art. Remember to add extra binder when diluting the paint with water.

Experiment with all aspects of the way you apply paint. Once you have explored the abilities and limitations of a watercolor brush, you might attempt different styles. Try holding the brush different ways and tilting the board in various positions. Experiment laying the color on thickly, in blotches, for a deliberately muddy effect. Inevitably some of your experiments will be total failures, but others will transcend themselves and leave you surprised at your own skill—or luck, as the case may be.

OTHER METHODS OF PAINT APPLICATION

Finger Painting. Any chimpanzee knows that you don't need a brush in order to paint. Finger painting is crude, blotchy, imprecise, and—obviously—*messy*. But it is also fun and produces effects that cannot be obtained in other ways. The consistency of undiluted Versatex is ideal. We suggest you avoid finger painting with oils not only because of the greater difficulty of washing up afterward but because many oil paints caution against prolonged contact with the skin. They can be a health hazard.

If you get bored painting with your fingers, you can always try painting with your toes or, indeed, your feet. This is how we produced our footprint T-shirt. Lay a generous coat of paint on your skin with a brush, patting the brush head rather than stroking it (thus avoiding brush marks). Then consider ways to touch up or further process your effects, using other techniques or media.

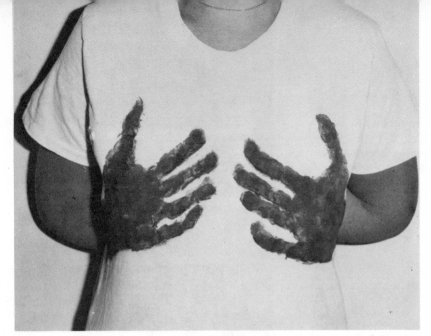

This T-shirt was hand painted—literally! Diluted water-base paint was applied to hands with a large, bristle, filbert brush with a patting rather than stroking motion. The results were then touched up, blending a variety of colors into the original reds and browns.

Foot printing (actually a form of block printing) may be a bit on the kinky side—but lots of fun! Diluted water-base paint was used, applied to the feet with a large, bristle, filbert brush. Many different parts of the body can be used for this sort of thing.

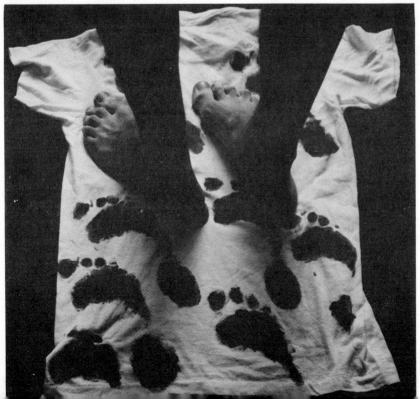

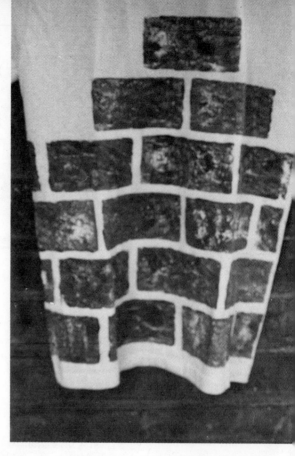

A simple block printing, using a brick, was executed in an oil-base paint diluted with an equal quantity of extender. The intentionally patchy texture lends itself to the subject.

Block printing. Footprints and handprints are crude forms of block printing, which we will define as coating a distinctively textured or shaped object with color and pressing it on the fabric to leave an imprint. To explore the real possibilitiies of this process, you can buy a set of linoleum cutters for about three dollars and use them to carve designs in small linoleum slabs sold at art supply stores (see Appendix). To ink the slabs evenly, a roller is required. Suitably diluted paint can be used, or you can try the ink that is specially made for the purpose. A distinctive shape or pattern can be repeated over the fabric; a simple example of this is our brick wall T-shirt, which was block-printed in oil-base paint from an oblong of embossed vinyl floor tile.

Block printing tends to produce uneven, patchy effects, but this random texture can be used deliberately (the brick wall shirt would have been far less effective if each brick had been solidly,

56

Two household objects were used on this block-printed shirt: half an apple and a coleus leaf. The apple prints were appropriately done in red fabric paint, the leaves in green. By Sandra Choron.

evenly colored). Look around the house for textured objects that will leave distinctive marks: a sponge, a cheese grater, a fly swatter, a steel wool or plastic pot scrubber. Use multiple colors. Dilute the paint more to create hazy backgrounds to be used behind other designs.

Homemade stencils. While chapter 6 is entirely devoted to letter stenciling, it is worth noting here that you can make your

Using paper stencils, undiluted water-base paint was applied to the center of this design, and diluted paint was used toward the edges. Magenta paint on a light blue shirt.

own abstract stencil designs. Our snowflake shirt is an example. Using tough, water-resistant rag paper, we cut three circles of varying diameters. Each circle was first folded in half, then the resulting half circle was folded into thirds, producing a wedge shape like a slice of pie. Using an artist's knife (for greater precision than is possible with scissors) nicks and oblongs were cut out of all three edges of the folded paper. When unfolded, the characteristic six-pointed snowflake shape resulted. Each shape was then used as a stencil, so that the paint penetrated the pattern of holes to produce the desired effect on the T-shirt. The paint was then heavily diluted to shade the background color off at the edges.

For long-lasting, completely waterproof stencils, we suggest you try using vinyl upholstery material. It is easy to cut and will

58

lie flat on the fabric. If you are working with an oil-base paint, test it on a sample of the vinyl first; some oil-base paints literally dissolve plastic.

Cut out patterns or shapes, such as stars, squares, circles, and wavy lines. Use each stencil several times over the fabric, with different colors. It is not necessary to attach the stencil to the fabric while you are working. Simply anchor it with your free hand. Allow some of the shapes to overlap, so that the colors overprint one another, resulting in new shades. Experiment! Stenciling is the exact opposite of block printing, in that the holes in a stencil produce the color on the shirt, whereas gaps, hollows, or parts that are carved away on a block correspond with uncolored areas when the block is printed. With some experience and trial and error, you will learn which designs are easiest to execute with either process.

Spray painting. When we talk about spray painting a T-shirt, we are *not* talking about the cans of household spray paint sold in hardware stores. That paint is generally not at all permanent and washes out easily.

To spray-paint fabric, you will need to use fabric paint, very heavily diluted, in an airbrush or similar spraying device, such as a plant mister. Unfortunately, fabric paints tend to be thick in consistency, and spraying works best with very thin-textured paint. Even heavily diluted, fabric paint tends to clog spray nozzles.

Oil-base paint can be diluted with denatured alcohol, but this is highly toxic, and although it produces a more workable mixture than any made with water-base paint, we cannot recommend it. To experiment, we recommend using a water-base paint such as Versatex, diluted with water and binder and applied with one of the small spray cans used to spray water on plant leaves. These sprayers cost only one or two dollars, whereas a commercial airbrush will cost twenty or thirty times as much.

The sprayer might tend to clog up, the paint droplets will vary

Stencils and spray paint were used to create this rather impressionistic painting of New York City's skyline. The Top Stop, New York City.

from a fine mist to a mess of raindrop-size blobs, and you will need to work either outdoors or, if indoors, with all the furniture covered to protect it from drifting spray vapor. The potential rewards, however, are great. If you can master the spraying technique, you will be able to produce gentle, soft gradations of tone unobtainable with any other process. Colors can be faded off to nothing or gently merged into other colors; stencils can be used to produce hard, precise edges. But it will take a lot of practice and multiple applications of the diluted paint to achieve any density of color.

A word of caution: Even when using the relatively safe, nontoxic, water-base paint, you should avoid breathing paint vapor or allowing it to get in your eyes. When working indoors, use a face mask.

Markers Versus Paint

Paint is much more versatile than markers. There are a half-dozen different ways of applying it, each offering opportunities to mix and blend shades of color, and each producing characteristic different effects. Paint is also cheaper, bearing in mind the amount of ink you buy for seventy cents or eighty cents or more in a single marker. Paint has more covering power than marker ink and is usually more permanent.

On the other hand, markers are easier to use than paints and more convenient. No brush technique is involved. The ink dries almost instantly, removing most worries about smudging one's work. There are no mixing dishes to be cleaned up afterward. Most important of all, markers are capable of generating fine, precise lines and outlines that are difficult or impossible with paint.

We think that the beginner should use markers because of their convenience and simplicity. But in the long run they serve best as an accessory to paint and to the other processes described in this book.

Crayons

Crayon coloring is another technique available to the T-shirt artist. Although the crayons have artistic limitations as far as color selection is concerned, their simplicity makes them highly recommendable for children.

Crayola Craft offers a set of fabric crayons for about eighty cents. While the kit includes only eight colors, black being an obvious deletion, we find that the crayons can be supplemented with marker pen colors after the crayon coloring has been

Crayon design by Lisa Drate.
Ironing for permanence by
Mrs. Drate. (*Photo by
Slawomir Dratewka.*)

completed. The drawing is first done on paper and then transferred to the shirt through an ironing process, which the manufacturer describes fully in the enclosed instructions.

Pentel Dyeing Pastels offer a greater range of colors (fifteen), which are applied directly to the fabric. The set sells for about $1.75 and is bound to last through a number of T-shirts. The permanency of the crayon design is activated by ironing, and again, the manufacturer has included easy-to-follow instructions for their use.

62

5

A DYEING ART:
Tie-Dyeing

Tie-dyed T-shirts were the height of fashion in the sixties, and although they are not as common as they were in their heyday, variations of the basic theme still play an important part in contemporary fashion and T-shirt art. Some of the less obtrusive patterns (especially marbling) are ideal as hazy, misty backgrounds over which a completely new design may be created in the foreground (for example, a painted bird against the patchy blue of a cloudy sky or an animal against the mottled green of a jungle scene). And the more distinctive tie-dyed patterns—veined splashes, regular squares and stripes—can be outlined and enhanced with other media (glitter, embroidery, silk screening) to produce wholly new effects that were never fully explored while tie-dyeing was in vogue a decade ago.

In addition, we shall deal with two variations of the tie-dyeing principle: tie-bleaching and tie-spraying. Each produces its own unique effect.

Choosing Designs

It is possible to create representational designs—leaves, outlines of faces—by painstakingly stitching the desired shape into the fabric before dyeing. This requires a fair amount of skill and practice to achieve successful results. However, we assume that tie-dyeing will mostly be used either to act as a blurred

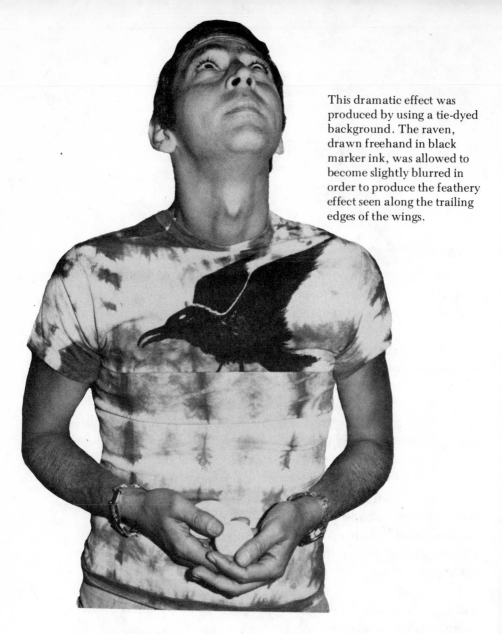

This dramatic effect was produced by using a tie-dyed background. The raven, drawn freehand in black marker ink, was allowed to become slightly blurred in order to produce the feathery effect seen along the trailing edges of the wings.

background or to stand alone as a simple abstract pattern. The available patterns are described in the section on techniques, since each pattern results directly from the particular tying technique used. Chance always plays a part in tie-dyeing, and until you are quite familiar with the process, we recommend not planning the exact design you want to achieve. Such plans are liable to be met with disappointments.

Designs suitable as foreground subjects, with tie-dyeing forming the backdrop, include most outdoor subjects (animals, people, buildings) or fantasy subjects (dragons, dream images, science fiction monsters). Produce your tie-dyed effect first, then decide what would look best with it.

Preparation

For the T-shirt to absorb as much dye as possible, it should first be washed in detergent to remove fabric sizing. Wrinkles should be ironed out. Thorough drying is unnecessary, since the garment must in fact be wetted before being immersed in the dye.

You will need strong twine (sisal twine is ideal) for the tying, or white thread if you will be using a sewing technique. Spread newspapers where the dyeing will be done; spilled dye is hard to clean off even smooth surfaces, such as kitchen countertops. If dye is spilled, apply bleach to it immediately; use diluted bleach to clean dye from hands.

We suggest using an aniline dye such as Tintex or Rit, which is sold in packets weighing about two ounces. Use half a packet per approximately two gallons of water. It is preferable to use a metal bucket to contain the dye solution, but if none is available, a very large saucepan can be used. There should, however, be free space around the tied T-shirt to allow dye to penetrate evenly.

Tying Techniques

The principle is that dye will be unable to penetrate to areas of the fabric which have been knotted, tied, folded, or sewn in a regular pattern, and these areas will thus remain uncolored. The tighter the fabric is constricted, the harder it will be for dye to penetrate. In addition, tying tightly produces sharper patterns and requires longer immersion in the dye.

65

Different methods of constricting the fabric include bundling up; twisting and coiling; knotting; concertina folding; and sewing. To gain experience with the techniques, we suggest you try them on scrap fabric, preferably white cotton, measuring about eighteen inches or two feet square.

BUNDLING UP

The fabric is crumpled into a ball by pushing from the edges toward the middle. Try to make sure that the fabric crumples in a regular, even pattern. Compress it gently and use thread to contain it, winding the thread around and around as if making a ball of string. Leave a long loose end of thread that can be used to pull the ball of fabric out of the dye. Because this method does not constrict the fabric tightly, dyeing should be brief—a minute may be sufficient. The result will be a random pattern of blurred

The bundling-up method of tie-dying produces this marbled effect. The fabric was immersed in dye three times, increasing the dye strength each time to vary the intensity of the pattern. The T-shirt was untied, rebundled, and retied between each dying. Each immersion lasted for only one minute. Thread was used for tying.

shapes, known as marbling. Since the exact effects are unpredictable, be ready to rebundle and dye the fabric some more or apply different dyes in succession to produce multiple color combinations and superimposed patterns, often creating illusions of depth.

TWISTING AND COILING

Stretch out the dampened T-shirt, pick it up from one end, and bunch the fabric together to form a narrow, ribbed tube shape. Tie one end with twine, exerting as much force as possible to be sure the fabric is tied tightly. Now twist the length of the T-shirt as if you were wringing water out of it. When it has been twisted tightly, tie the bottom end with string, then bring the two ends together. With some encouragement, the twisted fabric will wrap around itself like a skein of wool. Use carpet thread wound around and around the length of the fabric to hold it in this form. Immerse the fabric for about five minutes at first; longer immersion may be necessary, depending on how tightly you tie the T-shirt, and how much penetration of color you

The twisting and coiling method of tie-dying.

This effect was produced by twisting and coiling the fabric. Twine was used to tie the fabric, producing horizontal breaks in the vertical streaks. If thread had been used instead of twine, the streaks would have appeared unbroken. First the T-shirt was immersed in dye for five minutes, and then untied and recoiled to expose new areas. The shirt was then retied and immersed for fifteen minutes to add darker streaks. Red dye on a bright yellow T-shirt.

desire. The tighter you tie, the longer you dye. Dyeing produces soft-edged patterns, like a rain-streaked window pane, with some regularity to the effect.

Pick up the dampened T-shirt from a point in the middle of the chest area, holding the garment through just one thickness of the fabric. With your free hand smooth down the fabric that hangs from the point you are holding. Now tie a knot in the T-shirt near the top point. Subsequent dyeing will produce a mottled white splash where the knot was. Extra knots can be added in a regular pattern around the first knot. The fabric has to be knotted tightly, although when working with T-shirts there are limits to how tight a knot can be produced without permanently stretching or damaging the cloth.

The effect produced by knotting. One knot was tied in the chest area of the T-shirt and one in each of the sleeves. The shirt was immersed in dye for ten minutes and stirred frequently to ensure even application of dye to the large unknotted areas. Red dye was used on a green T-shirt, producing a green and brown color-mixed effect.

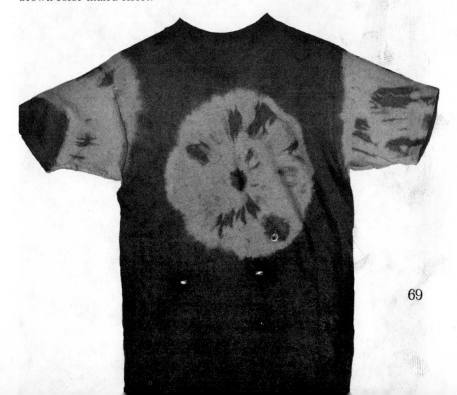

Variations of this technique all produce patterns that are defined and obtrusive. Soft-edged patterns and delicate shadings of tone do not generally result. The simplest concertina fold is a version of the simple knotting technique previously described. The dampened T-shirt is picked up in the same way, held from one point. Instead of the fabric being knotted, it is tied tightly at intervals down the dangling tube of cloth, using twine. Alternatively, thread can be wound around in a spiral. Constrict four or five inches of the fabric in this way. Dyeing produces a blank splash on the chest area, with veins of color radiating out from the center to the edges. Concentric white circular bands result if twine is used to tie the fabric at separated intervals. The more

Having been folded vertically in half, this T-shirt was diagonally folded concertina fashion into a three-inch wide strip. It was then tied tightly with twine and dyed for half an hour. The white stripes correspond to the positions of the tying twine. By Ava Sterling.

carefully the fabric is picked up and smoothed before tying, so that its folds are even and regular, the more perfectly circular the resulting pattern will be.

To produce tie-dyed stripes, the T-shirt is folded, concertina fashion, into vertical lines, making a long, thin strip about three inches wide. This is tied as tightly as possible at intervals along its length using twine. Immerse in dye for half an hour or so. Vertical stripes with occasional horizontal breaks will result.

A herringbone pattern can be achieved with a variation of the concertina-folding technique and is particularly suited to T-shirts. Fold the T-shirt in half vertically, along a central line from the middle of the neck to the middle of the bottom hem. Then concertina fold *diagonally* in three-inch strips across the fabric. Tie at intervals along the resulting shape or use a continuous spiral of thread.

Experiment with different patterns of concertina folding, remembering that the parts of the fabric folded inside and sections that are tied are the areas that will be protected from the dyeing process.

SEWING

Theoretically, any simple shape can be achieved by sewing its outline into one thickness of the cloth with a running stitch. Sketch the shape you wish to create, then use finger and thumb to pinch up the fabric into a *ridge*, following the contours of the shape. Sew through this ridge, using a running stitch, making it tight and permanent. The fabric will tend to bunch up, but this is not important. After dyeing, the result should be a white outline where the fabric had been constricted by sewing. For more interesting effects, sew several concentric patterns, each line following the shape of the one outside it. Or sew outward in radial lines, to produce effects such as the veining of a leaf.

The Dyeing Process

So far we have mainly considered the business of constricting the cloth to produce different patterns. There is less skill involved in the actual dyeing of the fabric, but some simple guidelines are necessary to guard against common mistakes.

First boil the water; this is liable to take longer than you expect, since such a large volume of water is used (two gallons per average dye bath). Then check that the T-shirt is thoroughly damp, which is necessary for the cloth to pick up dye evenly.

Pour about one ounce of aniline dye in the boiling water. Stir the dye bath with a large spoon to make certain the powdered dye dissolves completely. Then dunk the T-shirt. Leave it in for up to half an hour if it is tightly tied; much less time if the tying is looser. Stir the dye bath again while the T-shirt is immersed to make sure that all areas of untied fabric are equally exposed to the color. Avoid breathing fumes of the simmering dye.

Remove the T-shirt, with tongs or by the loose end of string from the tying. Be sure to have newspapers around the dyeing area and a bottle of bleach handy in case there are any spills. Rinse the T-shirt very thoroughly under cold running water for as long as necessary to wash out surplus dye, then untie, rinse some more, and hang up to drip dry. (Or retie right away if you plan to superimpose a second color on the first.)

Dispose of the used dye by pouring it directly down the sink drain, remembering that spills and splashes may be troublesome to remove.

Tie-Bleaching

Some colored T-shirts are quite vulnerable to bleach. Red T-shirts, in particular, are easily affected (red dyes always tend to be less permanent than other colors). Experiment by purchasing a selection of colored T-shirts made by various manufacturers. Dampen the fabric first, pour a little bleach into a small bowl, and dangle the garment so that just a tip of the hem is immersed. If no color change is visible in five minutes, remove the T-shirt, rinse, and repeat the process. If no color change is visible after another five minutes, or if the color fades very slightly, the bleaching process is ineffective on that particular color and brand of T-shirt. Give up! Set it aside to be used in some other process.

Garments that *are* affected by bleach can be tied in any of the methods described in the first section of this chapter and bleached by immersion for five or ten minutes. The fabric must be wet before immersion, and the tying should not be too tight; bleaching is not as potent an action as dyeing white fabric. The effects will be similar to tie-dyeing but easier in that no water is to be boiled, a large bucket or saucepan is not needed (only the tied areas are immersed in the bleach; the rest of the T-shirt is left out of the liquid), and the process is quicker. Remove the T-shirt after a few minutes of immersion, rinse it, and reinsert it to effectively speed up the bleaching action. Heating the bleach will also help, though this produces unpleasant and undesirable fumes.

Tie-bleaching can be used toward the same ends as tie-dyeing but is also useful for simply creating a soft-edged white area on the front of a colored T-shirt. A design can then be painted or inked in this area and will show up far more clearly than if it had been imposed on the color of the untreated fabric.

Tie-Spraying

Spray-painting fabric that has been colored, wrinkled, rumpled, or otherwise constricted in some regular way will produce pleasing patterns with soft gradations of tone, quite different from tie-dyed effects. Tight tying is out of the question, since spray paint has virtually no penetrating power and the thread or cord used for the tying will itself leave a white shadow when removed afterward. Instead, the technique is to lay out newspapers (over a wide area, since spray paint tends to drift) and fold or rumple the garment on the paper so that it will keep its constricted form with a minimum of assistance. A single piece of string tied loosely around the shirt is the most that should be required.

The steps in tie-spraying a shirt.

A. Rumpling the shirt prior to spraying.

B. The T-shirt after spray paint has been applied.

A pleasing, random pattern is produced if the T-shirt is gathered as described in "Bundling Up" (p. 66). The cloth is pushed in from the edges, gentle wrinkles being created. Each hump in the fabric should be about equal in size to the others. The resulting rumpled T-shirt should be about one quarter the

C. The cumulative effect of successive sprayings, similar to marbling by the tie-dyeing method.

size of the T-shirt stretched out flat. Spray paint is applied from a distance of about six to eight inches evenly over the face of the rumpled cloth. The paint is allowed to dry, then the fabric is smoothed out and rerumpled in a new pattern. Another spray color is applied, and the process is repeated as many times as desired, colors overlapping in different combinations. Use pastel shades; deep or strong tones will look garish and produce a dark, muddy effect where they overlap. Several different shades of one color (a variety of pale greens and blue greens, for instance) will be very effective for creating a mottled backdrop over which a foreground subject can later be superimposed.

Oil-based fabric paint (Prang) diluted with denatured alcohol can be used in a sprayer, but be careful not to breathe the vapor for long, and always work in a well-ventilated room or, even better, outdoors. For an easy clean-up job, Versatex fabric paint diluted with water can be used in a sprayer. See the section on spray painting on pages 59–61 for a discussion on the use of diluted Versatex fabric paint for spraying. This is probably your best bet.

Other tying, bundling, and rumpling techniques will produce other effects when the cloth is sprayed. As is the case with most of the processes described in this book, there is ample room for experimentation. Try out every method you can think of, using scrap cloth for trial runs. You may end up with a texture or effect totally different from anything that can be obtained with existing processes. You will then have a design that is not just your own work, but a result of your own inspiration.

6
SPELLING IT OUT:
Lettering

Words can be a small part of a pictorial T-shirt design. Or they can stand alone, especially if a decorative style of lettering is used. This chapter discusses the various ways of producing sharp, clean, professional lettering, beginning with the easiest methods and ending with techniques that require more skill. (For information on nonalphabet stencils, see the discussion in chapter 4 of block printing, pp. 56–57).

While this chapter deals with the task of getting the words onto the shirt, remember that the medium can be the message. After you choose your statement, ponder it awhile before you prepare your paints or inks. Does one method of T-shirt decoration especially lend itself to the words? "I Live to Boogie," for instance, might be best executed in glitter. And what better way is there of producing Dorothy's favorite T-shirt, "There's No Place Like. Home," than with colorful, down-to-earth embroidered letters?

Stenciling and Tracing

By far the easiest way of spelling out your message is to use a stencil-lettering set. They are cheap (usually less than a dollar for a complete alphabet) and come in a range of sizes and styles. Use a set of letters two inches high for T-shirt work unless the words

Simple stencil lettering using two-inch roman, plastic, stencil letters made by E-Z Letter (see Appendix). The T-shirt was painted with undiluted oil-base paint.

that you plan to stencil are very short, in which case a larger size will fit.

Stencil-lettering sets are stocked by most art supply stores, and you may even find some in your local five and dime store. In addition, the Appendix lists mail-order suppliers that carry stencils. Try to buy a set made out of plastic, rather than the old-fashioned, supposedly waterproof cardboard, which soon becomes limp and ragged with use.

Almost as easy as stenciling is tracing letters. You can trace the sample alphabets illustrated here (pp. 82–83), or you can seek your own in newspaper headlines, record album covers, and magazine covers. Your samples will most likely lack a few crucial letters, but with some experimentation, you can construct these yourself from segments of the other letters. For example, if you need an *X*, you can make it by tracing the top half of a *Y*, turning it upside down, and tracing it again underneath. An *F* is easily made if you have an *E*; a *D* can be made from a letter *I* and a letter *C* reversed; and so on.

If you are going to be doing a lot of lettered T-shirts, it may be worthwhile to make lasting copies of your favorite alphabet styles in ink on heavy paper. These can then be used as originals for tracing; they will last longer and be easier to use than a collection of scraps of newspapers and magazines.

PREPARING THE T-SHIRT

If you are using stencils, prepare the T-shirt as if for paint, using a large backing board inside the garment (see pp. 28–30), and add some newspaper between the board and the fabric to absorb surplus paint. If you have traced lettering onto paper, transfer the image to the T-shirt with the carbon paper technique (see p. 20). It will then be easiest to fill in the outlines with permanent marker ink, since a marker is easier to control precisely than a paintbrush. If you are using markers, omit the layers of newspaper that are required between the T-shirt and its backing board when using paint.

The slight horizontal stretch in the fabric caused by pulling the T-shirt over its large backing board will distort your lettering slightly, but in practice, provided the stretch is even, it will not show when the T-shirt is worn.

STENCILING TECHNIQUES

First, make a rough copy of the words you want to put on the T-shirt. On small sheets of tracing paper, use a pencil through your lettering stencils to reproduce rough outlines of the letters. Put each word on a separate piece of paper, making sure to leave at least a quarter of an inch between each letter and its neighbor. (Paint sometimes spreads slightly after it has been applied to

Planning the message. After sketching the stenciled words on individual slips of paper, move them about on the T-shirt until you find the most pleasing arrangement.

fabric, and ample space between letters make them more legible than if they bleed into one another.

Once you have seen how much space each word will take up, juggle them around for the best layout. Your message can be centered (each word aligned so that each one has its midpoint on a vertical, center line) or they can read across your shirt from left to right. Pin the words to the T-shirt in the position you think is best and hold the shirt on your chest to make sure it looks right. Remember that if your message is a long one it should begin approximately three inches below the neckline. A short message should be placed about five inches down.

All that remains, now, is to apply the paint or ink* through the stencil to the T-shirt. But this is the hardest part. First, take precautions to make sure your string of letters will be straight and even, rather than wobbling up and down like a crawling snake. Use a long ruler or straight piece of wood as a guide, and draw the faintest possible pencil lines (with a 2B or 3B pencil) across the fabric for each line of words. (This cannot be easily erased, but should come off the first time you wash the T-shirt.) Each stenciled letter must be positioned so that its bottom just touches the guideline. Round letters, such as *O, C, U, S,* and *Q,* can overlap the line a little, projecting a fraction below it, to look visually correct.

*See chapter 4, "Laying on Color," for a complete discussion of choosing paint and marker ink for your T-shirt designs.

80

It is important to apply the same amount of paint to each letter, so that an even effect is produced. If you are using a paintbrush, choose a bristle filbert (a so-called stencil brush is more difficult to use). Load the brush freshly with paint for each new letter, and using your rough sketch as a guide to placement, stroke *in* from the edges of the stencil. *Do not use too much paint!* Any excess will tend to creep out under the edges of the stencil, no matter how firmly you hold down the stencil on the fabric. In our experience, oil-base fabric paints are slightly easier to use with stencils than water-base paints; the latter should be very slightly diluted with binder, to achieve the ideal working consistency.

After experimenting using stencils and paint brushes, we discovered an easier way of applying paint. Take a scrap of suede or chamois leather about three by eight inches, turn the edges in, and roll it up into a little parcel. It can be held together with a few stitches of strong thread or paper clip wire. This object, a little larger than the ball of your thumb, will pick up paint but will not absorb very much. It will always tend to carry about the same amount of color (once it has become wet with the paint) and will apply it in neat dabs through a stencil. Having no stray bristles that tend to splay out and creep under the edges of the stencil, the leather pad is much easier to use than a brush. If water-base paint is used, the pad will easily rinse clean under a faucet.

The last pitfall of stenciling that should be mentioned is the tendency to smudge letters that you have just produced. A lot of patience is needed; you must wait until each letter is reasonably dry before applying the stencil to the fabric again for the next letter. Oil-base paint dries superficially faster than water-base; either can be expedited with a hair dryer. As a final precaution, you can place absorbent scrap paper or blotting paper over the lettering as you go along.

There is nothing particularly difficult about producing stenciled lettering. We have stressed our cautionary remarks only because stenciling is basically so easy that you may be

ABCDE
FGHIJ
KLMNO
PQRSTU
VWXYZ

These alphabets (*above*: Omnibus bold; at *right*: Hobo) can be traced from the page directly onto fabric.

ABCDE
FGHIJK
LMNOP
QRSTU
VWXYZ

Painted design with stenciled lettering by Lynda West. ©1974 by Lynda West and Charles Stettler.

tempted to rush ahead without any caution at all, spoiling your own work in the process.

After you have completed your first job, examine it critically. Is the paint too thick, too thin, smudged, blurred? Could different colors have been used? Is the letter spacing wide enough and regular? Consider whether the effect might be more interesting if you make the lettering follow a regular curve, rather than a straight line.

When cleaning up after a job, don't neglect the stencil itself. A residue of paint quickly builds up around the letter openings and should be removed as much as possible, before it dries.

If you are not working directly through a stencil, we suggest you assemble your complete message on sheets of tracing paper (one sheet per word). Use carefully measured guidelines to be sure that the letters are aligned. Then the whole thing (minus guidelines) can be transferred to the T-shirt with the carbon paper technique (see pp. 20–21).

Inevitably, in the tracing and then the transfer of the image, some inaccuracies will creep in. Straight lines will be not quite straight, curves will look a little uneven, and the thickness of the

Painted design by Lynda West. The lettering was copied from an Art-Deco typeface typical of the depression era. © 1974 by Lynda West and Charles Stettler.

letter strokes may vary. Try to compensate for these errors when you ink in or paint the lettering.

If using markers, begin with a fine-point marker and go around just the edges of each letter. Turn the T-shirt frequently so that your hand tends to rest on the center of the letter, with the tip of the marker pointing out toward the edge of the letter. Make a preliminary line just inside of the actual boundary of the letter; wait to see if the ink will spread in the fabric. Remember, you can always extend the edge of a letter outward, but you can never reduce a letter that grows too fat. If you make one too big, your only hope of saving the design is to go back over the rest of the letters and make *them* larger, too—a boring chore that is not recommended.

Once you have outlined each letter, it can be filled in. Obviously, a broad-tipped marker is quicker for this, though a medium point will suffice. We have found it possible to produce both sharp outlines and evenly filled-in areas with the medium-size point of a Sharpie marker.

If you are using paints, we suggest a medium-size, bristle filbert brush for the long straight lines and curves of letters and a small watercolor brush for putting in the little curves and corners. Even with good brushes and slightly thinned paint, the job is not easy. After the paint has dried, it will probably look blotchy and uneven, requiring a second coat in some places. And it will be hard, even with a good, small watercolor brush, to produce sharp corners and accurate curves within curves. But if you are able to master the brush technique involved, the painted result will be far more solid and satisfying than anything produced with markers.

When the job is done, examine it critically. Is it regular and balanced? If you used markers, should you have employed a ruler for the longer straight lines in the letters? Would a different layout look better?

As always, experimenting is the only way to achieve original results. Just try to make your experiments on paper *before* you start on the fabric.

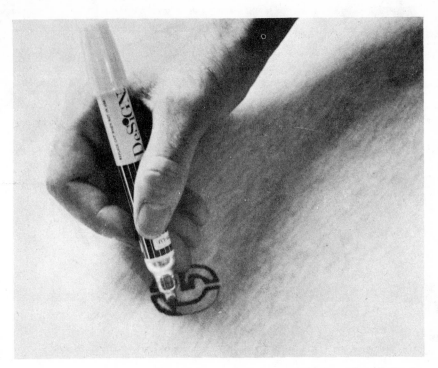

When using a marker to fill in a stenciled letter, the marker tip should always point away from the center of the letter to its outer edge.

Hand Lettering

Hand lettering, or sign writing, is as much a skill as carpentry or pottery making. The letters all have to look the same size, the same shape, and the same thickness; the tolerance for variation is surprisingly small. Any slight shake or twitch of the hand will irrevocably spoil the effect, and the stretchability of T-shirt fabric makes the job still harder.

But some lettering styles are easier than others, and you should at least experiment a little with hand lettering before settling for less. As a start, just try to notice the incredible variety of letter forms around you. Look at the lettering used on storefronts, trademarks, magazines, advertisements in newspapers, posters, books, TV commercials, headlines, typewriting—the list is endless. Notice that some common characteristics are shared by

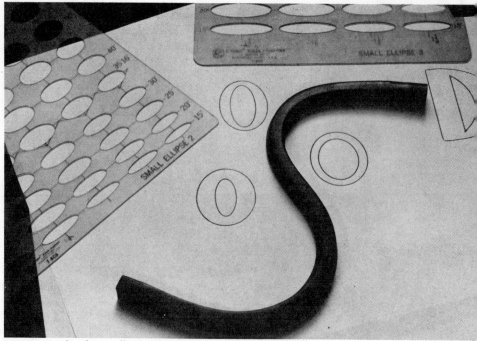

Lettering aids: plastic ellipses stencils and a flexible curve.

almost all lettering. The vertical strokes are usually thicker than horizontal strokes (dating back to when lettering was produced with an italic pen). Often the lettering slants forward (to the right) slightly. Many samples, including most typefaces used to print books, have their vertical strokes capped with little "feet" known as serifs, and in fact, all typefaces can be divided into those that have serifs (such as the one used in this book) and those that are "sans-serif," without serifs. The serif was originally introduced by stonemasons, since it made it easier to cut a letter in stone without splitting or flaking the stone at the ends of the letter strokes. The style has persisted because many people find it pleasing; there is no hard evidence that it enhances legibility.

Make a little collection of lettering styles that you like and try copying them. Accurate work can only be done if you lay down a pair of horizontal pencil marks, marking the upper and lower boundaries of your letter forms. When you think you have made a fair copy of some lettering, hold both the original and your version up to a mirror; this reversal will often reveal inconsistencies you failed to notice.

For precise lettering, you could consider buying a set of ellipse guides from an art store. Each is a plastic sheet with ellipses of various sizes and shapes cut out of it. Since most curved block letters (O, P, R, for example) conform approximately to the ellipse shape, and since curves are the hardest part of lettering,

"Smoking is Cheaper Than Long Life," claims this painted shirt. The border is especially interesting and was created with simple straight lines set in an imaginative pattern. The kooky lettering was done freehand. ©1974 by Lynda West and Charles Stettler.

the ellipse guides could save you some trouble. For large letters (1½ inches high and up) try using a flexible curve. This is a plastic-covered length of soft metal that bends into any shape you like, always producing smooth, even curves that are free of the kind of irregularities and errors that you will tend to make when sketching a curve freehand.

Once you have some ability in simple lettering, think about dressing it up. Buy a comic book and look at the incredible variety of hand-lettered styles that are used for dramatic effect. Explore the ways that letters are made to look three-dimensional, are distorted, are stretched or condensed. Lastly, think about the effects of color. Add black outlines and shadows. Put pale lettering against a strongly colored background, and vice versa. Keep sketching, and use tracing paper or thin typing paper to copy your own work, leaving out the errors, modifying it a little each time, until it looks perfect.

PREPARING THE T-SHIRT

The T-shirt should be laundered first to remove any sizing in the fabric which might interfere with the permanence of your design.

Whether you are using markers or fabric paint for hand lettering (markers are actually easier, in this case), you should stretch the T-shirt over a Masonite backing board, as described on pages 28–30. Center the shirt as best as you can on the board and avoid any distortions in the fabric. Several thicknesses of newspaper should be placed between the board and the underside of the fabric to be painted in order to absorb surplus color.

HAND-LETTERING TECHNIQUES

Develop your lettered design completely on paper, the same size that it will appear on the T-shirt, and then transfer the image with the carbon paper technique (pp. 20-21). When

Hand lettering taken to the point where legibility is sacrificed for the sake of producing a unified, integrated effect. Divisions between letters are so narrow that paints were considered too imprecise for this work, and marker pens were used, despite the relatively large areas to be covered. In dark blue, green, brown, and orange on a pale blue shirt.

filling in the letters on the fabric with markers or paints, the same remarks apply as have already been made about filling in traced lettering (see pp. 85–86). One additional caution must be mentioned; since you will now be filling in your own design of lettering, as opposed to a tracing of someone else's lettering, you may be tempted to "improve" on your design at the last moment, as you apply the ink or paint. Well, last-moment improvements are liable to become last-moment disasters. It is better to develop your lettering thoroughly on paper, be sure that it is exactly as you want it, then follow it faithfully.

Creative hand lettering is much more than plain print. Letters can shift and change like living things; they can be big and fat, tall and thin, imposing or discreet, garish or tasteful, strong and ugly, or delicate and beautiful. The basic shapes can be distorted

Some samples of hand lettering in a wide variety of styles, mostly frivolous.

an amazing amount and still be legible. They can even be overlapped and interlocked with one another (see our Zoot Money's Big Roll Band T-shirt). Lettering can become an obsession in itself, or it can just be a utilitarian way of putting a message across. Whether you choose to letter your T-shirt as ornately as a tapestry or as plainly as a newspaper headline is up to you.

7

SEWN-ON TRIMMINGS

Anyone who can thread a needle can add a few, simple, sew-on trimmings. The simple stitches are not difficult. The two things to be borne in mind when stitching items onto a T-shirt are: Don't stitch too tightly, since T-shirt fabric tends to stretch and will bunch up and pull out of shape if the thread drags on it too much; and don't add too much nonstretchable material, since the garment has to give a little when it is put on and taken off. Adding nonstretch fabric inhibits this ability and ripping of stitches or the fabric itself, will result.

Having mentioned these two cautionary notes, we can take off and explore the amazing range of possible trimmings and stitches that are available, every one of them making your T-shirt more distinctive, more obviously homemade, and more your own.

Hand Sewing

Many items are not easily sewn on with a machine, and others are better hand-sewn than machine-sewn because the former technique allows more accuracy and control, especially when adding small items and going around finnicky shapes.

We suggest you use colorless nylon thread for most of the ideas itemized in this chapter (with the exception, of course, of embroidery, where the thread itself is the design). Nylon thread stretches a little and is thus more compatible with the stretchable T-shirt fabric, and it is unobtrusive when used to sew on anything from sequins to patches.

DECORATIONS

Browse through a large trimmings store and discover the possibilities. You will find sequins, rhinestones, beads, all kinds of glittery stars, ovals, diamonds, pendants, leaves, and hearts, ready-made embroidered patches ranging from small rainbows to six-by-eight-inch pictures of animals, machine-stitched glitter and sequin designs that just need a few tacking stitches around their edges to be incorporated on the garment, fancy ribbons, strings of rhinestones and sequins, and even feathers!

It's easy to get carried away and be an impulsive buyer, grabbing a lot of items that catch your fancy at the time. When

A sample of the endless variety of sew-on trimmings available.

Painted, glittered, rhinestoned, and trimmed T-shirt by Lynda West. (*Photo by Tibor Schwartz*.)

you get home, however, you're liable to begin wondering what kind of T-shirt design could possibly incorporate all these different pieces of decorative whimsy. We suggest the precautions of planning out a few T-shirt designs in advance, making rough sketches, and then going to the trimmings store to buy items that will fit in one of your sketches.

What designs are suitable? For sew-on glittery items we suggest abstract patterns—curves, splashes, borders. Try to concentrate the sequins, rhinestones, or whatever in close-spaced groups or lines; spacing them out always results in a sparse, mean effect and is a false economy. Don't assume you need to cover a large portion of the total available fabric; a purposefully positioned touch here, a line there, and a shape linking them can be quite effective, especially when you use color intelligently. Most decorations come in a variety of colors and look best when they are applied to fabric that is itself colored. Silver glitter on a white T-shirt is not going to appear very exciting, if indeed, it is visible at all.

Techniques? Individual sequins have to be secured with individual stitches; no way around that, unfortunately. But with nylon thread a single stitch should be sufficient for each item and can be run on behind the fabric to the next sequin in line, as shown on the front cover of this book. Sew-on rhinestones have to be secured rather like buttons, but, again, just one or two stitches are sufficient. Alternatively you can consider buying rhinestones that clip into the fabric and are quicker to apply; see chapter 8 on Threadless Trimmings.

To secure patches and machine-made sequinned shapes, stitch gently around the edge of each item, allowing as little thread as possible to show, and spacing the stitches not more than a quarter inch apart. If holding the decorations in place while they are being stitched on is a problem (pins are often impossible to use with decorations), consider using just a little dab of white glue, such as Elmer's. This will wash out after the sewing has been completed but will hold the item fairly firm during the sewing process.

96

Lastly, if you use nylon thread, take extra care to knot the thread securely. It has a habit of unknotting itself.

We use this term to describe fabric shapes and designs that you cut out and stitch to the T-shirt, the fabric forms often overlapping. If you have no scraps of cloth squirreled away, ask around; a friend or a friend-of-a-friend or (almost without fail) an elderly relative is likely to have a whole hoard of bits and pieces of fabric that she or he couldn't bear to throw out. You can buy scraps of fabric cheaply at remnant sales or at five and dime stores, which enable you to purchase fabric in quantities as small as ⅛ of a yard. The mail-order firm of Reichert's Fabrics, listed in the Appendix, also has available a fabulous selection of fabric scraps sold especially for appliqué.

Assemble as big a selection as possible, then spread the swatches out and pick colors and patterns that go well together. Avoid wool scraps and thick fabric that will be obtrusive; look for thin cotton. Avoid garish patterns and colors that shout for attention; the principle of appliqué is to put together fabric samples that lose their individual identity in a larger picture, like individual painted areas in a painting by numbers.

What designs are suitable? Consider simple landscapes, animal shapes, skylines, lettering, symbols. Unless you are using felt scraps (whose edges will not fray) remember that each exposed cut edge of fabric will have to be turned under to prevent it unraveling, and this turning under can be tricky with complicated shapes or sharp angles. Curves are also difficult; since folding under the edge of the fabric tends to result in straight lines no matter how hard you try to persuade it to conform to a continuous rounded shape. Iron-on binding, available in most sewing supply stores, can make the job easier, though.

If you are inexperienced at appliqué, we suggest you choose a simple geometrical design to begin with—the kind of pattern often found on patchwork quilts, for example. To guard against

Appliquéd T-shirt. The hills are random fabric scraps of the kinds of patterns found on patchwork quilts. The house is a denim, iron-on fabric; the flowers in the foreground were cut from a patterned fabric and sewn on. The stars in the sky are studs, and the three-dimensional moon is embroidered in golden satin stitches. By Sandra Choron.

spoiling the T-shirt, the design can be put together using a separate piece of fabric as a backing; if the design works out well, the whole assembly can then be stitched onto the front of the T-shirt as though it were a ready-made patch.

You can plan out your design by executing it on paper first and then cutting templates out of cardboard. These can then be

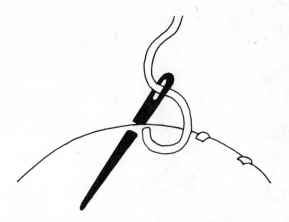

Blind-Hemming Stitch

Use the blind-hemming stitch to attach appliqué forms to a background or to other forms. Stitch the perimeter of the form using tiny stitches, picking up very little of the fabric as you go along. The stitches should be barely visible.

used to trace the individual elements onto the fabric. In most cases add from $1/8$ inch to $1/2$ inch around the design to serve as a hem. If you must use wool or velvet or other fabrics that fray easily, leave a larger allowance for hemming.

Once you have cut your form out of fabric, turn it over and fold down the hem of the shape. Iron the hem down, then baste it with a loose running stitch. Place it in its position on the T-shirt and stitch it down with a blind hemming stitch (see illustration). Try to get as close to the edges of the appliqué as possible, picking up very little of the background fabric as you go. The point is to wind up with a minimum of exposed thread. When you have attached the shape to the fabric, you can carefully pull out your original running stitches. Or you might consider leaving them in place as decoration. In this case, plan carefully the color of the thread you use. The edge of a scrap of fabric in the design need not be turned under if another adjacent fabric piece can cover it. Don't be afraid to overlap in this manner.

If there are a large number of elements in your design, you could consider stitching them together in advance of applying them to the T-shirt, using a sewing machine to save time. The advantage here is the wide range of stitches that might be available. See page 108 for the possibilities of machine embroidery.

99

Our Nouveau Pauvre shirt utilizes sew-on and iron-on patches randomly placed. The lettering was done by hand.

EMBROIDERY

The skill of embroidery has been the subject of entire books, and we do not intend to try to present a comprehensive guide to the techniques involved, any more than we could give a complete rundown on the general techniques of brushwork and use of color in our chapter on painting. However, there are some specific hints about embroidering T-shirt fabric, and the illustrations presented here will serve as a basic introduction to the possibilities of the technique. Beyond this, we suggest you turn to a book dealing exclusively with embroidery if you know little about it but want to pursue it in depth.

Simple embroidery borders only the neckline on this collared shirt. By Mary Jo Poole.

A variety of stitches make up the intricate embroidery of this traditional design. The colors are mostly shades of red, green, pink, and blue. By Frances Alter.

Back Stitch

The back stitch is the basis for many other embroidery stitches and can be used effectively for outlining. Bring the needle up at A. Insert the needle at B, and bring it up at C. To begin the next stitch, insert the needle halfway between C and A.

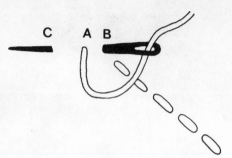

Cross Stitch

The attractive cross stitch, often found on old-fashioned samplers, is easily executed. Using the back-stitch principle, sew a row of slanted stitches, which will become half of the crosses. Then work back over these to finish the crosses. Neatness counts on this one!

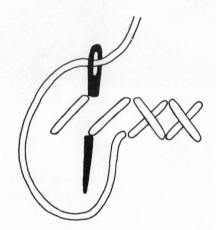

Long and Short Stitches

These stitches of alternating lengths are especially appropriate for filling in a large area. Rows of them, one underneath another, done in various shades of one color, can add an element of depth to your design. Using the back-stitch technique, keep the edges of the rows even.

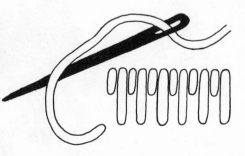

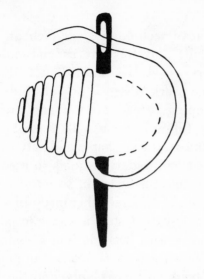

Satin Stitch

Parallel stitches are sewn beside one another to fill in a shape. For preciseness, draw the form on the fabric before you sew. Do not overlap the stitches or set them too far apart. Your finished form should lie flat. Satin stitches should not be too long lest they become loose and expose the fabric underneath. If you must fill in a large area, divide it up into smaller areas and work on them individually. Change the direction of the stitches from area to area for an interesting effect.

To create the padded satin stitch, which has a raised look to it, work a second layer of satin stitches over the first, working them in the opposite direction.

Stem Stitch

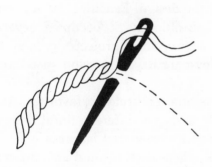

This is a good stitch for outlining, and it is advisable to chart your course with a dressmaker's pencil on the fabric before you begin. Work the stitches from left to right. Bring the needle up below the charted line. Insert it a bit further ahead, above the line, and bring it out next to the bottom of your last stitch. You may experiment with different lengths of stitches, placed closer together or farther apart, to create variations of the stem stitch.

Chain Stitch

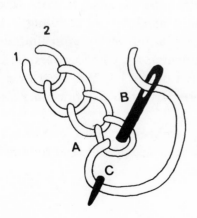

Create a loop with the thread by bringing the needle up through the fabric at 1. Hold the thread down with your thumb, leaving enough slack in the thread to make a loop. Insert the needle at 2. To make the next stitches in the chain, bring the needle up at A. Again, hold the thread down with your thumb to form the loop and insert the needle at B, bringing it out at C, allowing the loop to rest underneath the needle. C will be the starting point for your next stitch.

Probably no other decorative technique gives such an impression of care, detail, skill, and folk art as embroidery. Machine-stitched embroidery is always immediately distinguishable from hand-stitched work; there is no substitute for those painstaking hours looping thread around and around through the cloth, gradually filling in areas with lines of color that combine to form beautifully textured shapes and patterns.

No one would pretend that embroidery is quick to execute, and the area of a T-shirt is dauntingly large; so we strongly suggest you combine embroidery with some other medium when planning a design. Our ivy-on-a-gate T-shirt is a case in point. The wrought-iron gate was drawn first in black marker, freehand onto the fabric. The ivy was then sketched in pencil, working from pictures in a book on houseplants, and the embroidery was added last. The drawing of the gate took about one hour, including planning out the design. Penciling the ivy took another twenty minutes. Embroidering it occupied several whole evenings. When devising embroidery projects, try to make a little go a long way, at least until you develop speed and proficiency in the art.

Flowers and plants are perennial embroidery favorites. Any embroidery book will include a dozen different floral designs suitable for execution in thread. Embroidered lettering is fairly easy, and multicolored shapes where each colored area is fairly small are also ideal. The effect of embroidery is gentle and delicate rather than striking and bold, so choose designs accordingly. Avoid patterns that will involve very long stitches; these are easily damaged when the garment is worn (though longer stitches are, of course, a quicker way of filling in large areas). Consider embroidering a butterfly; your initials (in several colors with embellishments); a vase of flowers; a simple animal design, such as an owl or the head of a cat or a fish. Think about combining embroidery with paint or other media, such as glitter or tie-dyeing.

The technique of applying embroidery to a T-shirt is complicated by the stretchable fabric, which will tend to bunch up

This T-shirt combines a wrought iron gate done by marker pen with embroidered ivy. Designed by the author and executed by Marnie Whelan.

and wrinkle by the pulling of the embroidery thread. The stitches should not be too tight, and we find that to control this and make it easier to see how the finished result will appear, it is easier not to use an embroidery hoop. This could be a matter of personal preference, however, so feel ready to try it your own way.

T-shirt fabric is a fairly open knit, so it is quite acceptable to use embroidery thread in double rather than single thickness. This makes the design much quicker to execute and will also produce a bolder, easier-to-discern finished product.

The pattern you are embroidering can be laid down in soft pencil, or use light marker colors if you wish to make it as easy as possible to follow. Embroidery will entirely cover and conceal the fabric (unlike paint, for example, which is usually transparent enough to reveal what lies beneath); so you need have no

Embroidery serves as an attractive embellishment for hand lettering. "Sandy" was painted with diluted water-base paint, and all embroidery was done using the back stitch.

106

This familiar design was transferred to the T-shirt using the grid method of copying (see page 23). The long and short stitches and the satin stitches were sewn by Ilene Zeifman in fifteen different colors, emphasizing the intricacy of the design.

worry about marking the fabric too obtrusively when drawing your design.

Machine Sewing

There is less scope for machine-sewing designs on T-shirts than for hand sewing, simply because designs are unlikely to consist of simple straight lines that are easy to execute with a machine. We also feel that the handmade effect of hand sewing is more suited to T-shirt decoration than the mechanical effect produced by a

107

machine. There are just a few designs that are suitable for machine sewing, however, and we will itemize them.

We have previously mentioned that paint tends to be semitransparent, making it difficult to execute a light-colored design on a dark-colored T-shirt. The paint simply will not obscure completely the color of the garment, no matter how many coats are added or how much white is mixed in.

There is one very easy way around this, which is to paint the design on white fabric, then cut it out and stitch it on the face of a colored shirt. Obviously this method will be easiest if the design fits a square or oblong shape, but it should be considered for more complex shapes as well. To make the added panel unobtrusive, looking as much a part of the shirt as possible, machine sew its edges. Also we suggest you execute the design on a cotton knit as similar to the T-shirt fabric as possible so that its texture will look the same, and it will stretch with the T-shirt when the garment is put on or taken off. The added panel technique was used for our Paul McCartney T-shirt pictured on page 8 and the British Survivor shirt, page 135.

A sewing machine can also be used to add the pieces of cloth in an appliqué design, as mentioned in the section on appliqué.

MACHINE EMBROIDERY

If hand embroidering a design is too time consuming for you, and you own a sewing machine with a zigzag capability, consider trying to use the machine for embroidering, with the stitch length set to a minimum (so that the stitches fall close together) and zigzag at maximum (so that the strip of stitching is as wide as possible). Use embroidery silk if your machine will accept it.

Machine-stitching embroidery is fast but not easily adapted to filling odd-shaped areas. It is best suited to lines of color such as plant stems or filling in simple straight-edged areas. Practice a lot on scrap cloth before trying to work directly on a T-shirt.

Embroidered T-shirt by Singhtrade. The machine-sewn embroidery resembles satin stitches.

Machine-sewn embroidered T-shirt by Singhtrade.

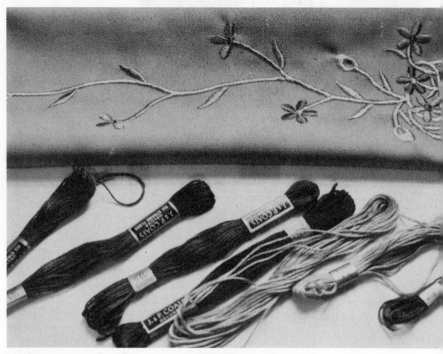

Machine-sewn embroidery.

If your machine can produce various special stitch patterns, you can experiment with these also as a decoration, but you may find that the thread patterns are too insignificant to show up when the T-shirt is viewed from any distance. However, don't forget to experiment with the possibilities of a free-flowing line.

When using a machine to embroider on T-shirt fabric, be sure to set the thread tension a little low, so that the fabric does not bunch up.

CUTTING THE T-SHIRT

It is natural to take the T-shirt on face value as a simple garment that cannot be very interesting so far as its shape and form are concerned. But you *can* "tailor" it, if you have enough determination and single-minded obsessiveness to do so.

110

Let us mention right at the start that working with the thin cotton knit fabric of T-shirts is not much fun. As soon as the fabric is cut, its edges curl over, and it is extremely hard to keep the overall shape of the garment from becoming grossly distorted. In addition, T-shirt fabric is not very strong, so that its stitches near a cut edge will tend to pull out.

On the other hand, there are few things more eye-catching than a plain, ordinary T-shirt that has been cut and tailored in some bizarre fashion; so if you want to be the sensation of a dress party, set aside a day or two, get out the scissors, and start chopping.

Spanish Rose, a long-sleeved white T-shirt, was cut from a point on the left shoulder to just under the right sleeve. The cut edge was reinforced with black lace. Black and silver rhinestones were inserted in the lower part of the shirt, and the red velvet rose completed the effect. By Sandra Choron.

Suitable designs should be simple. Avoid cutting complex shapes out of the fabric, and avoid cutting out areas that are very close to one another. Think in terms of inserting a few different panels around the edge, for example—wedge shapes that could make the T-shirt flare like bell-bottom pants.* Or insert lacy, semitransparent segments. Our lightning-bolt T-shirt (see page 148) goes all the way into the bizarre (and the obscene, some might say) by using a transparent plastic panel extending almost from neck to navel. The T-shirt edges that were cut were bound with cloth tape to prevent fraying, but even this presented problems, controlling the curling tendency of the knit fabric.

Cutting shapes out of the fabric is one thing; cutting the shirt to render it into another kind of garment is another T-shirt trip. To make our Spanish Rose shirt pictured on page 111, we started out with a long-sleeved white T-shirt and cut it diagonally from a point on one shoulder to a point beneath the sleeve on the opposite side to produce a semi-off-the-shoulder shirt. A string of red sequins holds up the cut end of the shirt. We used black lace to bind the cut edge and inserted some rhinestones at the bottom hem of the shirt. The red velvet rose on the shoulder completed the effect.

While the basic technique can lend itself to many themes, other cutting maneuvers are also possible. You might try removing the sleeves of an ordinary T-shirt and replacing them with long, flowing sleeves made of transparent silk fabric. You can cut a T-shirt just below the chest area to produce the very popular bare-midriff effect. Or slit the shirt down the front and sew in a fancy zipper. Cut the T-shirt above the chest area and sew on straps—made of anything from stringed sequins to fancy ribbon—to hold it up.

The intrepid seamstress or seamster can no doubt produce designs more ambitious than the examples we present here. However skilled you are, tailoring a T-shirt is liable to seem rather like producing a beautiful fine-line drawing on

*What an excellent way to transform your T-shirt wardrobe into a maternity wardrobe, should the need arise!

newspaper. It is stretching the capacities of the garment to the limit!

Hand sewing of cut-up T-shirts is not recommended because of the difficulty of handling the fabric and because close-spaced stitching is needed, due to the fabric's weakness. Provided the shirt is fed carefully into the sewing macine, we found no particular difficulty keeping it from bunching or distoring as it was sewn; on the other hand, this *has* been a problem in hand-sewn projects.

8

THREADLESS TRIMMINGS

There is a whole world of accessories and trimmings that can be glued or clipped on to a T-shirt without the use of thread. For those who never learned to sew or are impatient or simply find sewing a bore, consider the following.

Iron-Ons

Iron-on patches in a variety of sizes and colors are sold in stores ranging from sewing accessory specialists to Woolworth's. Buy the largest ones you can find and feel free to cut them into any shape you please to make symbols (stars, zodiac signs, cultural symbols) or easy lettering. To reduce the tendency of the patch material to peel off, try to use rounded corners in your designs wherever possible.

Using colored patch material to decorate your T-shirt has several advantages over paint or ink. Each shape is drawn and cut out separately, so if you make a mistake and spoil one, it can be thrown out, whereas if you make a mistake while painting a T-shirt the whole job is spoiled. The cut edges produce a very sharp, clean effect, hard to achieve with paint on fabric. And pale-colored patch material can be applied to dark-colored fabric, concealing it completely, whereas paint tends to allow the color of the fabric to show through.

114

Letter forms cut from iron-on fabric. A small package usually contains a good variety of colors.

Shapes were cut from patterned iron-on fabric and arranged in a typical patchwork quilt design.

Most iron-on patches simply require steady pressure of an iron for thirty seconds, set at 350 degrees. They are thus very quick and simple to use.

To execute designs, plan them on paper first. When you have decided which shapes to use, cut them out of the paper and use these as templates to cut the iron-on fabric. If you are cutting letters, review chapter 6, "Spelling It Out," for further instructions on planning your message.

One interesting way to explore iron-on patches is to fold the patch in half, then in half again, and use a scissors creatively to cut out bits and pieces of material. When the patch is unfolded, you will have a "snowflake," which can then be ironed to the shirt. A variation of the technique is to use those cutout bits and pieces (cut them larger, in this instance) and iron them onto the fabric in the kind of symmetrical pattern that is often found on patchwork quilts. The basic patchwork idea illustrated here hopefully will start you on your way to creating your own inspired designs.

Glitter

Most glitter consists of tiny flakes of shiny aluminum, naturally silver or anodized gold, red, blue, or green. Aluminum is slow to tarnish and the anodized colors do not fade; so you can rely on your glitter staying glittery through repeated washings and wearings of the T-shirt.

What you cannot rely on is the glitter staying attached to the fabric. Various glues advertise themselves as ideal for use on fabric, but in our experience hardly any of them hold glitter securely through even a single hand washing of the T-shirt. We have achieved best results with an adhesive *not* specifically designed for fabric—Scotch Multi-Purpose Spray Adhesive no. 6081, available in some art supply and hardware stores. This glue becomes tacky within seconds and sets to a rubbery but permanent consistency in a few minutes. It does not become brittle and will not wash out. It is a very pale yellow that shows

Silver and multicolor spray adhesive.

slightly on white fabric or pale blue fabric but is invisible on all other colors. A four-ounce can costs around two dollars and is sufficient to cover at least five moderate to large T-shirt design areas. Provided the instructions for use are followed, we find there is no tendency for the spray nozzle to clog, and any glue that accumulates where it isn't wanted (on the fingers, for example) is removable with turpentine.

The spray adhesive should be applied through a stencil or mask to limit the area covered. Absorbent fabric, such as is used in T-shirts, requires a slightly heavier coat of glue than is recommended on the can. Shake glitter generously over the glued area, immediately after spraying, then cover the glitter with a sheet of clean paper and rub hard to ensure adhesion. After ten minutes, pick up the T-shirt and shake it vigorously over newspaper to remove excess glitter that has not stuck. We then suggest you use an old toothbrush to flick off glitter that has adhered partially but not firmly. If you don't do this, the partially stuck glitter will come off soon enough when the T-shirt is being washed or, less conveniently, while you are wearing it.

The musicians on this shirt were painted by freelance artist Janey Fire of New New York City. Glitter was effectively used on the musical instruments. The painted design is black and gray; the glitter is gold and red; the T-shirt is white.

118

T-shirt painted by Lynda West using glitter highlights. The silver fabric stars were glued to the fabric with Duco cement. The lettering was stenciled. © 1974 by Lynda West and Charles Stettler.

Note also that glitter is hard to vacuum out of carpets and furniture.

Suitable designs for glitter should have rounded edges, no fine lines, and minimal requirements of accuracy. We suggest using glitter as an embellishment around designs executed in other media. Try glittery halos, galaxies, splashes, big star shapes. Avoid attempting to fill in fine lettering with glitter and similar projects where the glitter has to fit a specific area with defined edges. Some fineness of detail is possible if glue from a tube is used instead of the spray adhesive. The advantage here is that the glue can be poured into a small bowl and applied to the fabric with a paintbrush to produce fine lines. Unfortunately, we have been unable to find a tube glue that is as successful as the spray. Without wanting to seem wedded to Scotch brand products, we recommend Scotch Super Strength Glue as best of the six or seven glues in tubes we have tested, but it is still not as good as the Multi-Purpose Spray Adhesive.

Another product, which we discovered quite by accident, is a clear nail polish containing glitter. We used one manufactured by Helen Neushaefer. Available in a small but adequate range of colors, it is easily applied with a brush, dries in minutes, and won't wash off in the course of a normal hand washing. Although the glitter within the mixture is a bit sparse and the covered area does not sparkle as much as one might hope, its unique permanence makes it highly recommendable.

Our conclusion is that glitter is best reserved for fancy-dress-type garments which will not be frequently worn. It provides a gaudy, unique way of highlighting designs but is simply not practical for T-shirts that will be frequently washed or worn daily. Then again, as the artist of your own masterpiece, you can always summon your own command performance after each laundering.

Rhinestones and Studs

These are a much more permanent, durable way of achieving flashing, sparkling effects. The cost can add up, especially figuring in the eight dollars or more for the purchase of the gadget known as a nail-head setter to reduce the labor of fixing the decorations in fabric. But the results are impressive above and beyond almost any other decorative technique.

Rhinestones are available in many sewing supply stores, five and dime stores, and are sold also in some "head shops" in small bags containing an assortment of colors. You might consider buying one of these bags just to try out the product and the process, but if you are intending to use rhinestones in any substantial quantity, it will be worthwhile ordering them direct from a wholesaler. A retail bag of assorted rhinestones will contain perhaps twenty pieces and sell for three dollars; for the same price a wholesaler will sell you a gross (144). Check the Appendix for the addresses of suppliers.

Rhinestones are manufactured in two different forms. The simplest to apply are those in the form of a glass stone and

A small sampling of the selection of rhinestones and studs available.

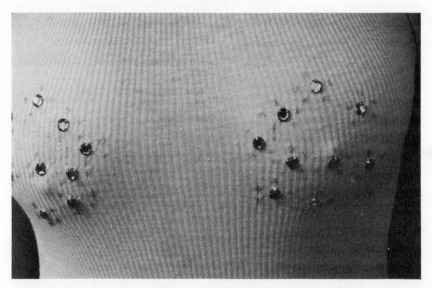

Simple rhinestone-studded shirt, decorated in the fashion of cabaret costumes. Pink and lavendar rhinestones on a lavendar shirt with nail-polish glitter used for highlights. By Sandra Choron.

separate metal back. The back, usually made of brass, has sharp prongs that are pushed through the fabric from the inside to the outside. The stone is then placed between the prongs, which can be bent around it using a screwdriver blade, a coin, or similar lever. These disc-backed rhinestones come in two sizes: 20 (small) and 34 (large). They are available in a wide range of colors. Their disadvantage is that the metal prongs bent around the stone sometimes tend to come unbent, whereupon the stone drops out.

The more durable type of rhinestone is a one-piece form called a preset; the stone is already mounted, and the mounting's metal prongs are pushed from the outside of the fabric through to the inside, where they are turned over to hold the stone in place. Presets are mounted in steel as opposed to the brass that is commonly used for the two-piece, disc-backed type; they are made in a much wider range of sizes (12, 16, 20, and 34) but a very limited range of colors. The form of their mounting and the use of steel instead of brass make them extremely permanent but very difficult to apply without the use of a nailhead setter. They are much harder to find than the disc-backed type of rhinestone;

The Brisk-Set gadget for inserting studs and rhinestones.

A glitter heart on a rhinestone necklace demonstrates elegant simplicity. By Sandra Choron.

one company, the Brisk-Set Rhinestone Machine Company (see Appendix) seems to have a virtual monopoly on the supply and sells a minimum order of ten gross, which is liable to be more than needed by even the most enthusiastic T-shirt decorator.

Some two-piece, disc-backed rhinestones are made with steel mountings and are, as a result, much less vulnerable to coming open, losing the stone. Their availability in a wider range of colors and their greater ease of application to the fabric cause us to recommend them over other types of rhinestones.

Plain metal studs (properly known as nailheads) are available from the same companies that supply rhinestones and can be inserted in the fabric by the same mechanical gadget. They are made in silver and gold colors, come in various shapes, and are cheaper than rhinestones, costing perhaps one or two dollars for a gross.

Any design can be highlighted with rhinestones or nailheads, but the result is usually a little garish and flashy. Reserve their use for fancy items. They can be closely spaced to spell out names or messages in simple capital letters, like an electric newspaper; they can be used in abstract patterns of multicolored

123

glittering dots that shift and change as the wearer moves; they can be a sunburst on a cloudy day or lights in a city at night. We suggest using them against dark cloth and emphasize that the larger range of colors of the disc-backed type is well worth exploring to produce subtler, more pleasing effects.

An amusing sample project could be the creation of a T-shirt that looks like a motorcycle jacket: a white shirt painted dark blue or black, with white lines left showing the outlines of pockets, lapels, and zippers. (These lines could be painted in wax resist before applying the dark coat of paint; see chapter 9 on batik.) Add a motorcycle club logo on the back, perhaps in the form of a stitched-on segment or iron-on material, and use commercially printed patches (motorcycle brand names, beer brand names, anything else that fits the image). Then go wild with the rhinestones and nailheads to produce a result that is not necessarily tasteful but certainly striking!

Other projects using rhinestones could include outlining or highlighting appliqué; putting the stars in a starry night (perhaps you could do a faithful reproduction of the van Gogh painting by the same name!); forming a glittery sun in a painted or embroidered landscape picture; adding creepy red eyes (mail-order suppliers that carry those crazy movable eyes often used in craft projects are listed in the Appendix) to a snake or insect head; or simply making abstract patterns.

T-shirt fabric is not particularly strong, and large numbers of rhinestones concentrated in a small area can pull it out of shape. But this is the only limitation that has to be borne in mind while running riot with this most gaudy of all decorative trimmings.

9
WAXING ENTHUSIASTIC:
Batik

Do you want to wear a T-shirt that looks like a cracked stained glass window? Or like a chameleon wrapped in cobwebs? It can be easily done with batik, an arcane and ancient art that produces such effects naturally.

Batik originated in Indonesia. In its primitive form, a design was painted on cloth with wet mud. The mud was allowed to dry. As it dried, it cracked. A stain was then applied over the whole cloth. Areas that had been painted with mud were protected from the stain and remained uncolored, although cracks in the mud did allow some stain to seep through, forming a tracery of lines across the otherwise protected fabric. Finally, after staining, the mud was scraped and washed off to reveal the design in white against a colored background.

In its traditional form, batik uses hot wax instead of mud to paint an image that will protect the fabric from a subsequent application of dye. The wax is cracked, deliberately producing the tracery of cobweb lines that are characteristic of batik and are considered a desirable part of the design.

Several successive applications of dye may be made, separated by the tedious operation of removing the earlier wax and painting a new pattern in fresh wax. Areas that are protected by wax at all stages remain uncolored; other areas receive different combinations of dye according to when they are protected and not protected, and the different dye combinations produce a

The shape of the chameleon and branch was cut out of thin cardboard to form a stencil, through which Batikit, hot, precolored wax was applied. Wax colors were mixed to produce a brown for the branch. After dyeing and wax removal, a dark blue marker was used to outline the chameleon and draw in its mouth. Imperfections in the blue background dye were covered by applying water-base fabric paint, diluted with binder and extender. A paint roller was used to ensure evenness of color.

wide range of different colors. It is a hard process to visualize, since at each stage the area being painted with wax is the area that will remain *un*colored. It is also a chore to melt the wax, paint with it, then remove it, several times in succession. However, batik does produce beautiful effects that cannot be obtained any other way. The advent of new products—a wax solution that does not need to be heated and waxes containing their own dye, allowing simultaneous application of various different colors—make batik reasonably easy for the amateur, though still more time-consuming than painting.

Suitable Designs

Whether one paints with hot wax or the modern cold substitute, it is hard to execute any detail and impossible to allow any shading of color. Image areas should be bold and simple. Stars, circles, hearts, symbols, patterns, and graphic forms are fine. Any representations—animals, birds—must be stylized, and neat lettering is just about out of the question.

For your first attempt at batik we suggest you use no more than two dye colors to avoid confusion. Draw a succession of sketches representing the succession of steps that will be carried out on the T-shirt: first coat of wax, first dye application; second waxing, second dyeing. Use watercolor markers to test how one dye will look when superimposed over another.

Your choice of design is so much dictated by the technique of the batik process that we will be no more specific than this. Read on, see our examples and full explanation, and then you will be in a better position to decide what you want to paint.

Preparing the T-shirt

The T-shirt should be prepared as if for painting. Launder the shirt first to remove any sizing, and when it is completely dry, stretch the shirt over a Masonite backing board as described on page 29, making certain the area to be waxed is centered over the board. Slide some sheets of newspaper between the shirt and the board to pick up any excess wax. Before you begin, be certain to cover your work area as protection against a possible mess.

Batik Techniques: Colorless Wax

Traditional batik uses a colorless wax whose sole function is to protect an area of the fabric from a dye that is subsequently applied. We will describe the two possible wax solutions, hot and cold, which are fundamental to the successive steps of batiking: wax, dye, wax, dye.

For hot wax, any candle wax can be used, heated in a dish immersed in boiling water or a double boiler. Direct heat must not be applied, since the wax is liable to catch fire above 200 degrees Fahrenheit. The alternative, a modern cold wax solution, is much easier to use than the hot wax solution. Cold wax has a pasty consistency at room temperature and does not need to be heated. It dries in an hour or two and is subsequently easier to remove from the fabric than ordinary candle wax. Dorland's Textile Wax Resist is a brand we have used with success.

Before applying the wax to the T-shirt, decide on the shape of your initial design. It and any subsequent forms can be transferred to the fabric by any of the techniques described in chapter 3, "Getting It on Your Chest."

While hot wax is painted on with a brush, cold wax can be applied with palette knife, dry sponge, or one-inch house paintbrush. For both hot and cold waxes use a small watercolor brush to fill in detail and sharp corners. Alternatively, use a stencil to define the waxed area; this is the best way of obtaining a clean, neat result. The wax must be applied thickly and allowed to dry thoroughly, at which point the fabric can be flexed to and fro along lines where you wish to crack the wax.

Hot wax soaks into fabric sufficiently to protect both the outside and the inside, so that the cloth can be totally immersed

Cold wax resist was applied, allowed to dry, and then cracked.

in dye. But cold wax protects only the outside, and instead of being dunked in dye, the T-shirt must be coated with color on its outside only. To do this, diluted fabric paint is used (see chapter 3 for a discussion on using fabric paint properly), applied with a large brush or, better yet, a small foam roller. You can paint over the entire T-shirt or save some time by limiting the color to fill just a frame around the waxed design. A large square or oblong stencil made from stiff cardboard will give the painted frame area sharp edges.

Remember to paint over the waxed design, as well as around it, to allow color to seep down through cracks in the wax to produce the traditional batik effect.

After the paint has dried thoroughly (preferably overnight), the wax must be removed.

129

Silk-screen design with batik fill-in. By A. Ramos, The Top Stop, New York City.

Batik fill-in was used here with a silk-screened design. By Mally, The Top Stop, New York City.

If you use hot wax, it must be removed by the laborious technique of covering the waxed area with several thicknesses of paper towels, then ironing the towels, which absorb the wax melted by the heat. New towels are applied frequently until no further wax is picked up. But the process is never totally successful; some wax is left behind in the fabric, giving it a pleasing translucent look when held up to the light, but a texture that some people find unpleasant to wear next to the skin.

If you used cold wax, scrape off as much as possible with a blunt knife, then wash out the rest in *very* hot water. Again, it is almost impossible to get out *all* the wax. If you used water-base paint to color the fabric, you may fear the water will wash out the paint with the wax, since the paint cannot be heat treated to make it permanent until the wax has been taken out. (The wax will melt if ironed.) However, the heat of the water used to wash out the wax will itself help to fix the paint, and not too much should be lost.

With the wax removed, you should now have an evenly colored garment (or colored frame on the front of the garment) with a white design. The next step is to repeat the whole process, waxing a new area and applying a different color over the first color.

The drawing on page 134 shows a sample, two-color batik design. If you try it, the heart shapes are the areas that are painted with wax in the first and second wax applications, respectively. Note that the second waxed area overlaps where the first one was. Allow the wax to dry as before, crack it, then apply the second color on top of the first color, out to its edges. Here are the results:

• Fabric where the two applications of wax have overlapped will remain white, unpainted.

• Fabric where there has been *no* wax protection will pick up *both* coats of paint and appear as a color mixture.

• Fabric protected by wax number one but not covered by wax number two will pick up only color number two.

132

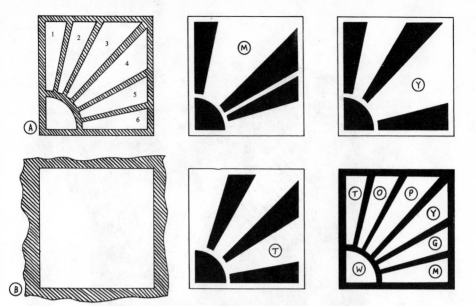

In this example, two stencils are used. Stencil A is a classic British art-nouveau design. The shaded areas are the paper, cardboard, or plastic from which the stencil has been cut. The white areas are the holes that have been made in the stencil material. Stencil B is simply a square cut out of stencil material; the square is exactly equal to the *outer* edges of stencil A. If A were placed in B, it would fit exactly.

In the diagram marked M, the black areas show where wax resist has been applied through the respective holes in stencil A. Counting around clockwise, only the first, fourth, and fifth areas have been used, plus the quarter circle in the corner. After the wax resist has dried (and has been cracked, if desired), magenta color is applied, using stencil B to limit the edges of the color. The magenta is applied over the *whole area*.

After the paint has dried and the wax resist has been washed out in hot water, proceed to diagram Y. Here wax resist is applied in bands one, three, and six of stencil A, plus the quarter circle in the corner. Then the whole area is covered with yellow paint, again using B to limit the area. Wash, as before.

Stencil T shows (with black bands) that segments two, four, and six have been coated with wax resist, plus the quarter circle. The area is then covered with turquoise paint, allowed to dry, cracked, and washed as before.

The last diagram shows the result: T = turquoise; O = orange; P = purple; Y = yellow; G = green; M = magenta; W = white. Orange, purple, and green have resulted from superimposition of the primary colors. The quarter circle has been protected by wax resist at all stages and thus has received no color at all. The black areas of the diagram show where all three primaries have superimposed on one another, forming a dark brown background. If the wax resist was cracked at each stage, each area of the design will be laced with a tracery of different colored lines over its principal color.

Note that the same effect could be produced in fewer steps by using the Batikit and simultaneously applying premixed colored waxes through the holes in stencil A and a background colored dye through stencil B. The result, however, would be less subtle and less interesting.

Simple two-color batik project.

• Fabric protected by wax number two but not by wax number one will pick up only color number one.

In our illustration, suppose that the left-hand heart shape was painted in wax first. Golden-yellow paint was then applied. Old wax was removed and the right-hand heart shape was protected with the second wax application. Then sky blue paint was applied. The final result will be a green background (yellow plus blue), blue heart segment on the left, yellow heart segment on the right, and a white area where the hearts overlap.

British Survivor, a batik-designed T-shirt, was produced in several stages.

1. The British flag was sketched on thick paper.

2. Areas to be painted in red and blue were precisely cut out with a knife, producing a stencil.

3. Red and blue paint were applied through the stencil onto a piece of white, cotton, knit fabric.

4. After heat setting the paint, cold batik wax was applied up to the edges of the flag. Scotch tape was used to mask off the fabric outside the edges of the flag.

5. The wax was cracked. Diluted black paint was then applied over the wax with a small roller.

6. The wax was removed. A cobweb tracery of black lines corresponded to cracks in the wax (the batik effect).

7. White areas that had been obscured by too much black paint penetrating through wax cracks were touched up with white paint.

8. The letters in the T-shirt title were cut out of heavy paper and placed in position, and a mask slightly bigger than the flag was placed over it to protect it.

9. Background color (orange) was applied with a roller over the entire area. Letters were then removed, leaving white shapes in the orange background. Where paint had crept under the letters, white was used to touch them up.

10. After heat setting the orange and white, the letters and flag were outlined in black by marker. The piece of cotton knit fabric was then cut to size, its edges turned under, and sewn onto a dark blue T-shirt.

11. The assembly was ironed one last time to insure color permanence and to smooth wrinkles caused by the sewing.

Things get even more complicated when three colors are used. The figure on page 133 shows the stages of a three-color design made with stencils, allowing different color combinations to accumulate in different areas. Visualizing the end result during the process is quite complicated. If you find it hard to understand the way that colors superimpose and if you dislike the long process of removing two or three successive wax applications, the one-step process using pre-colored wax may appeal to you.

Batik Techniques: Precolored Wax

The Batikit, made by the American Art Clay Company, contains wax that is colored and will transfer its color to the fabric as

The contents of the Batikit.

Batiked T-shirt. The simple shape was created with Dorland's Wax Resist and outlined in fabric paint. The design required only one wax application.

it is applied. In this system, different colors of wax can be applied to different areas of the design *all in one step*, and the color of the wax is the color that will remain in the fabric. A dark dye (also supplied in the kit) is used all over the fabric after the wax has dried and has been cracked; the dye forms a background color around the wax-colored areas and seeps through the wax cracks to produce the usual batik effect.

The main disadvantage of the Batikit system is that it does not use cold wax. The colored waxes have to be melted and painted on while they are in liquid form. There is a fire hazard (we do not recommend this for small children), and the brushes tend to clog up easily. There is also the extra trouble of removing the wax from the fabric after it has been applied hot; ironing over

137

paper towels is the only way, and some residue tends to remain, as noted previously.

Another disadvantage of the Batikit is its price. For around ten dollars, it includes a total of not more than five ounces of wax, four tin melting dishes, a packet of dye, two poor-quality brushes, squares of coarse-woven cloth on which to execute designs, and sample designs that the user can copy. By comparison, sixteen ounces of cold-wax solution does not cost much more than two dollars, and fabric paint used instead of dye in the cold-wax technique is also quite cheap.

The hot precolored wax method of the Batikit allows simultaneous application of many colors, followed by immersion in one dark dye and the rather tedious process of hot wax removal. The cold wax method involves a series of separate color applications, and a series of wax removals, but the cold wax is easier to extract from the fabric and much easier to work with than hot wax. It is also much cheaper than the colored waxes in the Batikit.

On balance we recommend the cold-wax technique, unless you have particular difficulty visualizing how successive separate color and wax applications will work out in the finished design.

10
SILK-SCREENING

Silk-screen printing is the process used to mass-produce almost all designs on commercially marketed T-shirts. Yet, it is well within the range of the amateur craftsman in terms of the expense and skill involved.

First it must be emphasized that any effect that can be produced with silk-screen printing can also be produced, usually with less trouble, simply by using a paintbrush and/or permanent markers. One of the advantages of silk-screening a design is that large numbers of duplicates of it can be turned out very quickly. If you ever become so involved with T-shirts that friends not only admire your designs but start asking you to produce similar items for them (and offer you payment for your work), silk-screening is the easiest way to satisfy their demands and start your own little printing business at the same time.

Another advantage of silk-screening, as you will learn when reading about the process, is the ease with which very intricate, fine-line drawings can be transferred to a T-shirt.

The Silk Screen: A Simple Stencil

The central part of the process is a rigid wooden frame over which is stretched a piece of thin, open-weave material, like cheesecloth but with larger gaps between the threads. Although this fabric is no longer made of silk, it is still referred to as such,

The liberated T-shirt. The Susan B. Anthony commemorative postage stamp was silk-screened onto the fabric by Bill Bailey of Mythology, New York City.

the whole assembly being the silk screen. Small ready-made screens can be bought in art supply stores. The frame and "silk" can be purchased separately, and you can stretch and mount the silk yourself, but we do not recommend this. The tension must be firm and absolutely even, which is difficult to do without experience. It is worth paying the few extra dollars for a ready-made screen as opposed to the raw materials for one.

The principle of the printing process is very simple. Areas of the screen are masked or blocked off, using plastic film or a gummy substance that effectively clogs the mesh. The open areas of mesh that are left constitute the design that is to be printed. The screen is clamped down over a T-shirt (like a stencil), and ink is spread evenly across the screen using a rubber squeegee made for the purpose. Where the screen has not been masked or blocked, ink penetrates easily through the open mesh and is

140

Silk-screened T-shirt by Bill Bailey of Mythology, New York City.

Silk-screened T-shirt by Bill Bailey of Mythology, New York City. A great amount of detail was successfully included in the transfer process.

deposited on the garment. Where the screen is blocked, no ink passes, and the T-shirt remains uncolored.

After applying the ink (which takes just a few minutes) the T-shirt is removed and another one can be put in place right away, to repeat the process. Further copies of the design can be made, limited only by the permanence of the method used to block out the design on the screen. One of these methods, the plastic film, will last almost indefinitely; other methods are limited to about fifty impressions, after which the image starts deteriorating.

The Plastic Film Method

This is probably the most popular method for laying out a design on the screen used by small printing enterprises today. Cutting the film requires skill and a very sharp, special, small-bladed knife made for the purpose, but the precise, clean-cut, printed result is worth it.

The film is laid over the design that you wish to have printed. The design will be visible through the film, which is usually colored but transparent enough for even small detail to be clearly seen. The knife is then used to copy the design onto the film, cutting through the plastic in the process. A transparent backing sheet between the film and the design holds cut portions of film, preventing them from coming loose; it takes a fair amount of practice to know exactly how hard to press with the knife to cut through the plastic, but not through the backing sheet as well.

When the design has been copied, the cut areas of film corresponding to the black areas of the design are carefully lifted with the knife point and peeled off the backing sheet. The film is then placed under the silk screen and held tightly in position. A soft rag saturated with adhering thinner is rubbed over the screen; the thinner partially dissolves a lacquer coating on the plastic film, softening it so that when it rehardens it has knitted into the material of the silk screen, holding the film in position.

The backing sheet is then removed from under the silk screen,

The dark outlines of butterflies were silk-screened onto this T-shirt, and the colored wings were hand painted in various shades of blue. By Mally, The Top Stop, New York City.

and open areas of screen around the edges of the plastic are filled in with a lacquer mixture that blocks the mesh. The screen is now ready for use.

This is an abbreviated description of the steps involved, and any reader interested in seriously pursuing silk-screen printing should read through the catalogs offered by the silk-screen suppliers listed in the Appendix.

Liquid Block-Out Methods

Occluding areas of the screen with a lacquer or glue, applied with a paintbrush, is easier in that the tedious and difficult

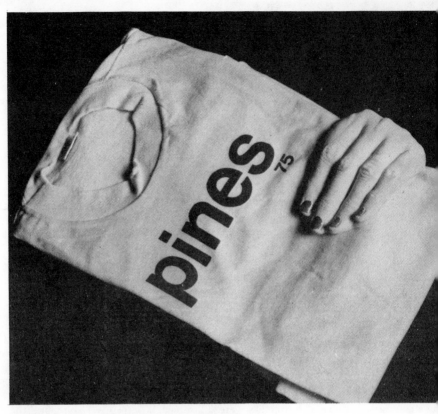

Simple silk-screened lettering by Russell Redmond.

process of cutting out a film is avoided. However, it is harder to execute detail using a brush; the blocked-out areas break down with the use of the stencil, limiting the number of copies that can be made with it; and the printed result is not as sharp as the one achieved with the plastic film method.

For simple liquid block-out of the screen, the design is placed under the screen and traced onto it with pencil. The design should be as simple as possible: bold lettering or a silhouette.

After the design has been traced, it is removed, and the screen is supported so that there is some space beneath it. A silk-screen glue or lacquer is then painted *around* the shapes that were black areas in the original design. When the glue dries, the screen is examined to see if the occluded areas are completely filled in. Any remaining pinholes are touched up. The screen is

144

then ready for use; ink will pass through the areas that were *not* painted with glue, and thus the screen will reproduce the form of the original design.

There are more sophisticated techniques of liquid block-out, but this is the general principle.

The Photographic Method

A design can be transferred to a silk screen photographically, using special chemicals and equipment designed for the process. Most commercially printed T-shirts produced in large numbers are created in this way.

The silk screen is coated with a chemical that hardens or becomes insoluble where light falls upon it. The design is then projected on the screen, using photographic equipment. The

Simple silk-screened design using six different colors. By Bill Bailey of Mythology, New York City.

design has to be in the form of a negative, like a photographic negative, where areas of black and white are reversed with respect to each other.

After exposure to the projected design, areas of the screen that were not subjected to light are washed clean of chemical, and the remaining blocked-out areas are treated to make them thoroughly permanent. The screen is then ready for use.

It must be emphasized that this is a simplified sketch of photographic methods of producing silk-screen designs. In reality the various processes are more complex and often require expensive equipment. For our purposes, it is sufficient to describe the general principles so that the reader has some idea of available techniques for anyone who wants to pursue silk-screen printing seriously.

Starter Kits

On a more practical level for the amateur, it is possible to buy starter kits containing all necessary materials for simple silk-screen printing, including a screen. We have seen and recommend a kit by Craftint (see Appendix), containing a fair quantity of colored inks, thinner, squeegee, nine-by-twelve-inch screen, and blocking-out film, which works on a variation of the principle previously described. This kit is adequate to give the reader a working knowledge of silk-screening and its possibilities. It should be added that the process is of course usable on materials other than fabric; it can be used to reproduce greeting cards, for example. It is also used by artists who wish to make and sell prints of their work. Silk-screen printing is not a very sophisticated process: Subtly shaded tones are extremely hard to achieve. But it is the only printing process that is easily within reach of the amateur, requiring an absolute minimum of equipment. For this reason, it is worth your consideration, even if you do not plan to mass-produce T-shirts.

11
MORE T-SHIRTING

We have included as broad a range of techniques as possible and have dealt with them in as much depth and detail as space allowed. But we can never claim to have tried *every* possible process and idea in T-shirt art; there will always be new variations on old ideas, new techniques, and new materials coming on the market. Some ideas that we believe are new and have not been used elsewhere have been incorporated in the relevant chapters; particulary tie-bleaching and tie-spraying in chapter 5. Other innovations that came to mind during the preparation of this book were not included because there was insufficient time to develop and test them properly. This chapter will pass on these half-developed and untried ideas to you, for you to pursue and perfect as you choose.

Paint Application. In chapter 5 we dealt briefly with block printing and paint spraying as alternatives to applying paint with a brush. But inevitably there were endless block printing possibilities we did not follow up. Anything you can press against fabric can be coated with paint to leave its distinctive mark, from squares of carpet to bicycle tires (remember "action painting" in the late fifties?), and the only limit is your own inventiveness. Where spraying paint is concerned, it occurs to us that a stencil that is deliberately shuffled around during spraying will produce a blurred, out-of-focus effect that might be pleasant as a background; spray that is applied obliquely to

This fancy costume was executed without ink or paint. One-inch blue and ½-inch magenta cloth tapes were stitched around the edges of a zigzag panel cut in the front of a bright yellow T-shirt. Clear plastic (from a cleaner's garment bag) was stitched into the opening, using long running stitches. Glitter was added with Scotch Multi-Purpose Spray Adhesive.

wrinkled (not crumpled) fabric will build up on the wrinkles, leaving white shadows below them, like a relief map; spray can be applied *through* objects such as fly swatters and pot scrubbers, producing a white silhouette of their texture; and to create the spray of paint, the kind of vaporizer used by pharmaceutical companies to squirt nasal decongestant spray might work better than the plant mister we suggested in chapter 4.

Wetted Fabric. We mentioned the wet-on-wet technique, where water-base paint is applied to a damp cloth, and spreads into the fibers producing a fuzzy effect. What would be the result if an *oil*-base paint were applied to fabric only dampened in patches? Would the paint stick only to the dry and partially dry areas of the cloth, producing a patchy, tie-dyed effect?

Wrung-Out Fabric. Imagine taking a T-shirt covered in diluted water-base paint, still wet, and twisting it, wringing it so that some parts would rub against other parts, and some areas (particularly the wrinkles) might lose their color altogether. The result might be a pleasing texture.

Paste and Paint. Paste could be mixed with water-base paint to create a texture as thick as mud, drying to a three-dimensional surface like an oil painting.

Batik Variations. Can a color pigment be added to Dorland (Cold) Wax Resist? Can this tint be persuaded to transfer from the cold wax into the fabric? If so, the result would use the best of the two batik processes described in chapter 9, combining the advantages of cold wax (easy application, easy removal) with the advantages of one-step colored wax.

And are there alternatives to wax? Rubber cement, for instance, could be used to make selected areas paint-resistant, and could perhaps be peeled off the fabric afterward far more easily than removing any kind of wax.

Self-Adhesive Stencils. Why not cut stencils from sticky plastic sheets such as Con-Tact, sold cheaply in hardware stores and

For the wet-on-wet technique, heavily diluted water-base paint is applied to thoroughly dampened fabric. The spreading of the paint in the fabric is intentional but can be arrested at any time by applying heat from a hair dryer.

Woolworth's? There would be no problem holding every part of the stencil close to the fabric; it would hold itself down. More detail could be used, and there would be hardly any risk of paint creeping out under the stencil edges.

The above is a random selection of ideas. Undoubtedly there will be more. There are hundreds of ways to create mixed media shirts, combining two or even five techniques described. We hope you will feel interested enough and creative enough to branch out into new experiments of your own, creating new techniques and new effects, adding to the range that we have covered in this book.

12
CARING FOR YOUR T-SHIRT

In our experience, T-shirts do not shrink. The white ones do not turn yellow, and the colored ones do not fade. What you have put on the fabric may be a lot more delicate than the fabric itself, however.

Tie Dyeing will not be fully permanent in hot water. Some fading can be tolerated (it will not show, since the effect is blotchy to begin with), but we suggest using a cold-water wash.

Marker Ink fades and runs more easily than any of the other colorings we have mentioned in this book. Wash in cold water with a minimum of laundry detergent. Hand wash if possible, since this is faster than a machine cycle. Then remove the water as quickly as possible (ideally in an extractor, such as are found in some laundromats) and immediately tumble dry. If you do not have access to a dryer, iron the fabric until the area that has been colored is dry. Do not hang the T-shirt up to drip dry; this will inevitably result in the marker ink bleeding slightly. Rather lay it out flat to dry.

Paints are generally fully permanent and can be washed in hot water, except where you have used water-base paint heavily diluted (which reduces its permanence) or oil-base paint mixed with a lot of white. Hand wash samples to test for permanence in these instances.

Embroidery does not generally shrink but may be damaged in the action of a washing machine. We suggest hand washing.

Glued-On Trimmings (studs, rhinestones, etc.) are likewise vulnerable to washing machine action. Glitter will tend to come off no matter what you do, unless you have used glittered nail polish. Hand wash with care, flexing the fabric as little as possible. Do not remove water in an extractor; this creases the fabric, tending to remove the glitter.

Silk-Screen Inks vary. Wash a sample if possible.

Aside from washing, be gentle wearing your T-shirt. Excessive stretching or abrasion will tend to remove paint and damage embroidery. Marker inks, unfortunately, are even more vulnerable to human persperation than to water and detergent; if you perspire a lot on a hot day while wearing a T-shirt decorated with markers, you may have the disconcerting experience of looking at your chest and seeing your design wilting before your eyes. Where paint is concerned, you need have no such worries—although *you* may be the one to wilt on a hot day, since paint clogs up the fibers of fabric and cuts off ventilation of your skin.

Overall, common sense and cold-water washing should safeguard any design and keep it fresh and bright for years to come. Even if it does get damaged or becomes faded, you will have one advantage not shared by anyone who wears store-bought designs. You can always take your old T-shirt, put it on the backing board, and start all over!

APPENDIX:
Mail-Order Crafts
Suppliers and Manufacturers

In case you find it difficult to fill your T-shirt needs, the following crafts suppliers fill mail orders. In many cases the listed outlets carry much more stock than we have mentioned; we have only included the products described in this book.

Art Mart, Inc.
31 N. Meramac
St. Louis, Missouri 63105
(314) 725-7858

Block printing, felt pens, screen process supplies, textile paints. Catalog: 25¢.

M. B. Austin
138 W. 25th Ave.
San Mateo, California 94403
(415) 341-5847

Patches, sew-on railroad patches. Catalog: 50¢.

Behnson Silk Screen Supply
   Ltd.
950 Richards St.
Vancouver 2, B.C., Canada
(604) 683-6951

Batik supplies, inks and dyes, screen process supplies. Write for information.

Bergen Arts & Crafts, Inc.
Box 381
Marblehead, Massachusetts
   01945
(617) 631-8440

Artist's supplies, batik, block printing, textile paints. Catalog: $1 (refundable).

Berry's of Maine
20-22 Main St.
Yarmouth, Maine 04096
(207) 846-4112

Swatches. Catalog: 10¢.

Dick Blick
Box 1267
Galesburg, Illinois 61401
(309) 343-6181

Artist's supplies, block printing, felt pens, screen process supplies, threads, yarns. Catalog.

Boin Arts & Crafts
87 Morris Street
Morristown, New Jersey
  07960
(201) 539-9040

Artist's supplies, batik, block printing, fabric paint. Catalog: $1 (refundable).

Arthur Brown & Bro., Inc.
2 West 46th Street
New York, New York 10036
(212) 575-5555

Artist's supplies, batik, block printing, felt pens, flexible curve rulers, screen process supplies, textile paints. Catalog.

Budget Buddy Co.
11141 Orchard Rd.
P. O. Box 9777
Kansas City, Missouri 64134
(816) 761-7657

Stencils, transfers. Catalog: $1 (refundable). Send SASE for transfer sample.

Delco Craft Center, Inc.
30081 Stephenson Highway
Madison Heights, Michigan
  48071
(313) 585-1678

Artist's supplies, batik wax, block printing, boutique trims, cold-water dyes, dyes, screen process supplies, textile stencils, yarns. Catalog.

Sam Flax
250 Sutter St.
San Francisco, California
  94108
(415) 391-7400

Artist's supplies, batik supplies, fabric paint, felt pens. Catalog.

Gail's Decorative Arts Studio
9602 S.W. 57th St.
P. O. Box 696
Olympia Heights Station
Miami, Florida 33165
(305) 271-9502

Rhinestone bandings, rhinestones, roses. Catalog: 25¢.

Gibsons Creations
4733 West Grace St.
Chicago, Illinois 60641
(312) 283-5232

Beadery, boutique supplies, rhinestone bandings, rhinestones. Catalog: $1.25.

Handcraft House
110 West Esplanade
North Vancouver, B.C.,
  Canada
(604) 988-6912

Dyes, yarns. Catalog: 50¢.

154

Holiday Handicrafts, Inc.
Box 470
Winsted, Connecticut 06098
(203) 379-3374

Boutique items, glitter, movable eyes. Catalog.

Home-Sew, Inc.
Bethlehem, Pennsylvania
18018
(215) 867-3833

Felt appliqués, metallic trims, movable eyes, nonmetallic trims, pearls, rhinestones, rickrack, sequins, threads. Catalog.

House of Gould
1290 N.E. 135th Street
Miami, Florida 33161

Dyes, needles, transfer pencils. Catalog.

House of Lines
P. O. Box 156
Kentfield, California 94904

Cotton patchwork quilt squares, felt remnants, velvet patchwork quilt squares. Catalog: 50¢.

House of Patterns
Box 39
Valley Park, Missouri 63088
(315) 825-2021

Embroidery designs, fabric paint, sewing, patterns for appliqué, quilting designs. Catalog: 50¢.

Koehler's Craft Outlet
205 South Boundary Ave.
Procter, Minnesota 55810
(218) 624-0743

Glues, ribbon, sequins. Catalog: $1 (refundable).

The Mail Train
4007 Bellaire Blvd.
Houston, Texas 77025
(713) 665-5599

Cotton threads, embroidery threads, needles. Write for information.

Thelma Sutton Martin
Cherryvale, Kansas 67335
(316) 336-2077

Stencils, textile brushes, textile paints, textile stencils. Stencil catalog: 60¢ or send stamp for design list.

Merribee
2904 West Lancaster
Fort Worth, Texas 76107
(817) 335-9413

Crewel, embroidery hoops, embroidery threads, needles, transfer pencils. Catalog.

Joan Moshimer
North Street
Kennebunkport, Maine 04046
(207) 967-3711

Accessories, batik, fabric dyes, wool swatches. Write for information.

New York Central Supply Co.
62 Third Avenue
New York, New York 10003
(212) 473-7705

Artist's supplies, batik supplies, fabric paint, felt markers. Catalog.

Northwest Handcraft House 110 West Esplanade North Vancouver, B.C., Canada (604) 988-6912	Batik dyes. Catalog: 50¢.
Nantucket Needleworks Nantucket, Massachusetts 02554 (617) 228-1913	Embroidery design transfers, embroidery threads, hoops, yarn. Catalog: $2.75.
Hazel Pearson Handi Craft P. O. Box 519 4128 Temple City Blvd. Rosemead, California 91770 (213) 443-6136	Batik, beadery, boutique ribbons, fabrics. Catalog: $1.50 (refundable).
Pins & Needles P. O. Box 2535 Hialeah, Florida 33012 (305) 685-2698	Carbon tracing paper, pattern paper. Write for information.
Plaza Artists Materials, Inc. 210 East 58th Street New York, New York 10022 (212) 759-7550	Artist's supplies, screen process supplies, tracing paper. Catalog.
Reichert's Fabrics 101 Nashua Rd. East Pepperell, Massachusetts 01437 (617) 433-2872	Corduroy scraps, cotton-polyester woven scraps, leather scraps, quilt scraps. Scraps are sold by the pound. Write for information.
Rub 'N Buff Box 68163 Indianapolis, Indiana 46268 (317) 293-5591	Batik kits. Write for information.
Rupert, Gibbon & Spencer 470 Maylin Street Pasadena, California 91105 (213) 792-0600	Batik materials, block printing dye, permanent brush-on dyeing. Catalog plus color chart: $1.
Sangray Corp. Box 2388 Pueblo, Colorado 81004 (303) 564-3408	Transfers. Write for information.
Sax Arts & Crafts 207 North Milwaukee Street Wilwaukee, Wisconsin 53202 (414) 272-4900	Alphabet stencils, batik, block printing, dyes, fabrics, glues, screen process supplies, stencils, stitchery, textile paints, wax, yarns. Catalog: $1.

Siphon Art Products
Durable Arts Division
74 Hamilton Drive
Ignacio, California 94947
(415) 883-9006

Batik wax blends, cold process batik textile wax, press block print makers, water soluble textile paints. Write for information.

Skil-Crafts Division
The Brown Leather Company
P. O. Box 105
Joplin, Missouri 64801
(417) 624-4038

Artist's supplies, boutique items, dyes, transfers. Catalog: $1 (refundable).

Lillian Vernon
510 South Fulton Ave.
Mount Vernon, New York
    10550
(914) 699-8881

Acrylic felt pens, appliqués, patches, studs. Catalog.

Walnut Hill Co.
Box 355
Huntingdon Valley,
    Pennsylvania 19006
(215) 947-6613

Adhesive sprays, glitter. Catalog: 25¢.

Lee Wards
National Office
1200 St. Charles Rd.
Elgin, Illinois 60120
(312) 697-3800

Beadery, boutique trims, embroidery threads, fabrics, rhinestones. Catalog.

Zim's
P. O. Box 7620
Salt Lake City, Utah 84407
(801) 262-5469

Boutique trims, fabric paints, fabrics, transfer pencils. Catalog: 50¢.

If the above list does not meet your needs, you can write directly to the manufacturers listed here for distribution information.

Batikit
American Art Clay Co., Inc.
P. O. Box 68163
Indianapolis, Indiana 46268

Brisk-Set Rhinestone Machine Co.
28 West 38th Street
New York, New York 10018
(*Also suppliers of brass disc-backed rhinestones and nailhead setter machine.*)

C & C Button and Trimming Co.
318 West 39 Street
New York, New York 10018

Design Marker
Eberhard Faber Pen & Pencil Co.
182 Second Ave.
New York, New York 10003

Dri-Mark Products, Inc.
Mount Vernon, New York

E-Z Letter Stencils
P. O. Box 829
42 Locust Street
Uniontown, Maryland 21157

M & J Trimming Co.
10008 Ave. of Americas
New York, New York 10018

Magic Marker Corp.
Glendale, New York 11227

Pantone, Inc.
55 Knickerbocker Road
Moonachie, New Jersey 07074

Prang Textile Paint
American Crayon Co.
Sandusky, Ohio 44870

Screen-A-Print Kit
Craftint Mfg. Co.
18501 Euclid Ave.
Cleveland, Ohio 44112

Siphon Art Co.
74-D Hamilton Drive
Ignacio, California 94947

Speedball Cutters (linoleum cutters)
Hunt Mfg. Co.
Statesville, North Carolina 28677

INDEX

Abstract designs, 48
Acrylic paint, 31
Alphabets, for hand-lettering, 82–83
Aniline dye, 65
   dyeing process, 71–72
Appliqué, 97–99
   highlighting, 124
Artist's knife, 58
Artists' oil paint, 31

Ball-point pens, 23, 32
Batik, 125–138
   colorless wax technique, 128-136
   cost of, 138
   disadvantage of, 137–138
   precolored wax technique, 136–138
   preparing the shirt, 127-128
   suitable designs for, 127
   variations, 150
Block painting, 56–57
Bristle filbert, 81
Brushes, 50–51
Bundling-up method of tie-dyeing, 66–67, 74
BVD T-shirts, 3

Carbon paper, for transferring design, 21
Care, washing and wearing, 151–152
Circular design, 16
Color mixing (for fabric paints), 49–50
Coloring, 31–62
   for beginners, 61
   block printing, 56–57
   crayon coloring, 61–62
   with fabric paints, 44–54, 61
   finger painting, 54
   homemade stencils, 57–59
   with marker pens, 33–44, 61
   spray painting, 59–61
   what not to use, 31–32
Colorless wax batik technique, 128–136
Concertina folding, 70–71
Crayola Craft (fabric crayons), 61
Crayon coloring, 61–62
Cross-stitch, 102
Cut-up T-shirts, hand sewing of, 110–113

Decorations, 94–97
Design Marker, 33, 36

Designs
    abstract, 48
    geometrical, 12–17
    op-art, 12–17, 48
    See also specific methods of
        decoration
Designs, transferring, 18–30
    carbon paper method, 20–21
    grid method, 23–25
    pencils for, 20, 21, 23, 30
    photographic method, 27–30
    stencils and templates, 22
    by tracing, 18–20
    using a pantograph, 25–27
Drawing ink, 31
Dri Mark, 33, 36
Dyeing process, 71–72

Ellipse guides, 89–90
Embroidery, 100–107
    hand, 100–106
    machine-stitched, 104, 108–
        110
    technique of applying, 104–
        105
    washing, 152

Fabric crayons, 32, 61
Fabric paints, 44–54
    brushes, 50–51
    color mixing, 49–50
    painting techniques, 49–53
    preparing the shirt, 49
    suitable designs for, 47–48
    using tracing paper with, 45
    Versatex versus Prang paints,
        45–47
Finger painting, 54–55
Fruit of the Loom T-shirts, 3

Geometrical design, 12–17
Glitter, 96, 116–120
    spray adhesives for, 116–117
    suitable designs for, 119
Glued-on trimmings, washing,
    152
Grid method, for transferring
    designs, 23–25

Hand lettering, 87–92
    alphabets for, 82–83
    ellipse guides, 89–90
    preparing the shirt, 90
    styles, 87–88
    techniques, 90–92
Hand sewing, 93–94
Hanes T-shirts, 3
Homemade stencils, 57–59
Household oil paint, 31
Household water-base paint, 32·
Hunt clips, 21

Ideas, getting, 7–17
    from the media, 7–11
    op art and geometrical
        designs, 12–17
    of self-expression, 11–12
Indelible copying pencils, 30
Iron-on binding, 97
Iron-on patches, 114–116

Jockey T-shirts, 3–4

Knotting technique of tie-
    dyeing, 69

Lettering, 77–92
    by hand, 87–92
    preparing the shirt, 79
    stenciled, 77–84
    stenciling techniques, 79–84
    tracing, 77–79, 85–86

Lines, drawing, 11-12
  geometrical design, 12-17
Liquid block-out (silk-screen)
  methods, 143-144
Long embroidery stitch, 102
Loop embroidery stitch, 103

Machine sewing, 107-110
  added panels, 108
  embroidery, 104, 108-110
Magic Marker, 33, 36
Marker ink, washing, 151
Marker pens, 33-44
  drawing techniques, 41-44
  filling in lettering with, 86
  ink base, 33
  nib styles, 34, 35
  preparing the shirt, 38-41
  shading with, 43, 44
  suitable designs for, 37-38
  tests and ratings (by brand
    name), 36-37

No. 199 Stanley knife, 22
Nylon, 4
Nylon thread, 93-94

Oil-based paint, 31, 59
Op art, 12-17, 48

Paint
  applying, 147-149
  washing, 151
  See also Acrylic paint; Fabric
    paint; Finger painting;
    Spray painting
Pantographs, for transferring
  designs, 25-27
Pantone, 33, 36

Paper clips, 21
Paste and paint, 150
Patches, 96, 114-116
Pencils
  for tracing designs, 20, 21, 23,
    30
  using with a pantograph, 25-
    27
Pentel Dyeing Pastels, 62
Photographic (silk-screen)
  method, 145-146
Photographic (transferring)
  method, 27-30
Photographs, tone reduction in,
  9-10
Plastic film (silk-screen) method,
  142-143
Posters, 48
Prang (fabric paint), 45-47
  for tie-spraying, 75-76
Precolored wax batik technique,
  136-138
Printers' ink, 32

Rhinestones, 120-124
  cost of, 120
  designs for, 123-124
  for outlining appliqué, 124
  sewn-on, 96
  types of, 120-122
Rit (dye), 65
Rubber cement, 150

Satin embroidery stitch, 103
Scotch Multi-Purpose Spray
  Adhesive, 116, 119
Scotch tape, 21
Self-adhesive stencils, 150
Sequins, sewn-on, 96
Sewing method of tie-dyeing, 71

161

Sewn-on trimmings, 93–113
   appliqué, 97–99
   cutting shapes, 110–113
   decorations, 94–97
   embroidery, 100–107
   by hand, 93–94
   machine, 107–110
Sharpie, 33–35, 36
Shopping for shirts, 3–6
Short embroidery stitch, 102
Silk-screen inks, washing, 152
Silk-screening, 139–146
   advantage of, 139
   liquid black-out methods,
      143–144
   photographic method, 145–
      146
   plastic film method, 142–143
   simple stencil process, 139–
      142
   starter kits, 146
Spray painting, 59–61
   for tie-spraying, 73–76
Stem embroidery stitch, 103
Stenciled lettering, 77–84
   pitfall of, 81
   techniques for, 79–84
Stencil-lettering sets, 78
Stencils
   lettering techniques, 79–84
   for silk-screening, 139–142
   for transferring designs, 22
Studs, 120–124
   designs for 123–124

Templates, for transferring
   designs, 22
Threadless trimmings, 114–124
   glitter, 116–120
   iron-ons, 114–116
   rhinestones and studs, 120–
      124

Tie-bleaching, 72–73
Tie-dyeing, 63–72
   bundling up method, 66–67
   choosing design for, 63–65
   concertina folding, 76–77
   dyeing process, 71–72
   knotting, 69
   preparation, 65
   sewing, 71
   techniques, 65–71
   tie-spraying, 73–76
   twisting and coiling method,
      67–69
   washing, 151
Tintex (dye), 65
Tracing (through the shirt), 18–
   20
Tracing design, 18–20
Tracing letters, 77–79
   filling in, 85–86
Tracing paper, 20, 45, 90
Transfer pencils, 30
Trimmings, 93–124
   sewn-on, 93–113
   threadless, 114–124
Twisting and coiling method of
   tie-dyeing, 67–69

Versatex (fabric paint), 45–47,
   59
   for tie-spraying, 76
Vinyl upholstery material, 58–
   59

Water-base paint, 32
Wetted fabric, 149
Words. See Lettering
Wrung-out fabric, 149–150